In DEFENCE *of* FREEDOM

Margaret Thatcher

In DEFENCE *of* FREEDOM

Speeches on Britain's Relations with the World
1976 - 1986

Introduced by Ronald Butt

Foreword by
President Ronald Reagan

Prometheus Books

Buffalo, New York

Published 1987 by
Prometheus Books
700 East Amherst Street, Buffalo, New York 14215

First American Edition.

92 91 90 89 88 87   5 4 3 2 1

Originally published in 1986 by Aurum Press, London.

The speech to the House of Commons (p. 143) is reproduced
from *Hansard*, vol. 77, no. 97, 16 April 1986.

All photographs are by Peter Jordan, with the exception of
those on p. I and p. II (top) which are © The Press Association.

Library of Congress Card Catalog No.: 87-60188
ISBN: 0-87975-401-X

Printed in the United States of America.

Contents

Note: Each speech is preceded by a commentary by
Ronald Butt.

PUBLISHER'S NOTE

The speeches chosen for inclusion in this book were selected by Mr Alistair B. Cooke, the Deputy Director of the Conservative Research Department.

All the speeches except one are printed here in almost exactly the form in which they were delivered. The single exception is the speech of 26 May 1982 to the Conservative Women's Conference devoted largely to the repossession of the Falkland Islands. Passages of that speech unrelated to the Falklands campaign have not been included.

A very small number of introductory comments expressing thanks to hosts and conveying good wishes have been omitted, along with, in certain cases, references to the individuals who presided over particular meetings where speeches were given. One paragraph of the speech to the United States Congress was omitted because it bears a close resemblance to a passage in an earlier speech. One or two other repetitions have been removed, but nothing of any substance has been left out

Foreword

President Ronald Reagan

In warfare, Napoleon wrote, the moral to the material is as three to one. Fierce in her belief in the primacy of ideas, Prime Minister Thatcher has included the quotation in this volume. I might add that it is because a similar ratio prevails in statecraft that the Prime Minister so excels in its practice.

Her personal strength has by now quite rightly become a matter of renown. There were the wrenching early years, when Mrs. Thatcher and her government set themselves the task of seeing to it that, for once, inflation should go *down*. Through it all, Mrs. Thatcher stood firm—and today inflation *is* down. There was the Falklands crisis—the Falklands crisis and Mrs. Thatcher's famous answer. Pressed on the point, she collected herself, smiled calmly, and simply replied, "Failure—the possibilities do not exist."

And there are, even now, the hostile sessions—the heckling, the harassment—in the House of Commons, at least once a week at the Prime Minister's Question Time (an ordeal I have never ceased to thank the framers of our own Constitution for sparing the President). Mrs. Thatcher can certainly become roused in these sessions when she needs to, but as I listen to the broadcasts, it seems to me that even then she retains a certain, unshakable inner confidence, even serenity.

This inner confidence arises, of course, from Mrs. Thatcher's convictions, among them the subject of this volume—the belief that human freedom is to be cherished, and defended. All her policies turn upon this one central point, and upon the crucial insight that it is not only *right* to defend liberty, but of immense practical *use* to the polity. Given freedom, Mrs. Thatcher holds, individuals will on balance behave responsibly and govern wisely. And given freedom, they will create jobs, goods, and services—in short, economic growth. It would be inappropriate for me to comment in detail upon the policies of a fellow Head of Government. But perhaps I could safely go so far as to suggest that they seem to have passed the only test that truly matters. They work.

In this collection, there is much to learn from, and much to enjoy. Reading it deepened my already immense respect for Prime Minister Thatcher as a leader—and made me still more proud to be able to call her a friend.

Introduction

In 1975, the Conservatives elected Margaret Thatcher as their leader, giving her a clear mandate for a fundamental change of direction in party policy and attitudes. The situation with which she had to deal was unprecedented in twentieth-century British politics, and it arose from the breakdown of the post-war consensus to which both the Conservative and the Labour parties had hitherto broadly adhered. The basis of this consensus had been created after 1951 by the legacy of the 1945 Attlee government, the first Labour administration to have an overall majority in Parliament. That government had been elected not as a result of any urge for Socialism in the British people, but because if offered policies which appeared to be remedies for what had come to be generally accepted as social shortcomings in pre-war Britain.

What the public mood demanded was a government which provided greater equality of opportunity; which saw to it that every citizen was assured of proper education, health care and pension arrangements, regardless of personal means; which established a safety net to deal with hardship; and which pursued economic policies for the revival of basic industries and the maintenance of employment.

These broad aims were shared by both parties; the argument was simply about the policies and system through which they should be implemented. For instance, it was R. A. Butler, the Conservative Education Minister in Winston Churchill's coalition, who had been responsible for the 1944 Education Act establishing the principle of equality of opportunity. That Act governed educational practice until, largely under the influence of left-wing thinking in the sixties, it was changed to a system putting emphasis on social engineering to promote a theoretical concept of equality. The idea of ensuring that each child had equal opportunity for the type of education to which he or she was best suited was lost. So was a proper concern for educational standards, to the increasing dismay of parents. Not until the Conservatives redirected public attention to the decline in standards was any serious effort made to counteract this, and in July 1986 the Labour Education spokesman, Mr Giles Radice, acknowledged candidly Labour's mistake in neglecting standards and so getting out of tune with parents who regarded it as the central issue in education.

Similarly, the Conservatives would also have legislated for national insurance arrangements to cover every citizen's health care and pension, had they been elected in 1945. The question was simply the means by which these aims were to be achieved. The Attlee government's solutions, based on Socialist principles, were to be the cause of great future difficulties. For example, the creation of a National Health Service with blanket provision of wholly free health care for all, regardless of means, and paid for overwhelmingly out of general taxation, was an open-ended commitment fraught with risks both for national economic management and ultimately for the quality of the health service itself. As medical procedures became more sophisticated and expensive, and demand for them increased, a burden was imposed on the Exchequer which did not only add to inflationary pressures. When the country was in economic difficulties, the need for cuts in government spending inevitably affected the quality of the NHS, and of other vital services. They all had to compete with less important claims on the shrinking public purse, with no proper system of priorities.

More generally, the neo-Keynesian principles by which the

economy was managed pushed governments to boost demand through inflationary spending and borrowing at the first sign of less than full, or over-full, employment. In a situation of high employment there were inflationary wage settlements, particularly in the public sector, and since Labour had nationalized many of the then basic industries, taxpayers' money had to be found to sustain them in the manner to which they had become accustomed, irrespective of commercial justification. At the same time trade unions used their strength both to extract more money without commensurate increases in productivity, and to force employers to agree to over-manning and restrictive labour practices. Steadily, British industry had become less competitive. Financial and balance-of-payments crises were a regular phenomenon as governments struggled to maintain the fixed parity of the pound when its real international value was slipping.

All this flowed from the abuse of the kind of mixed economy which was established as a result of the Attlee government. For the Conservative governments which followed, acting in accordance with British political tradition, had not totally reversed what their predecessors had done. They had instead attempted to improve and build on it, while enabling private enterprise to rebuild itself. So markets were reopened, the economy was liberated, and better financial discipline was sought for state industries and services. But since, for instance, the Conservatives would themselves have introduced a health service of some kind they did not wish to cause yet another upheaval by crudely uprooting the one they had inherited. Instead they concentrated on trying to improve it, and as with the social services generally, on trying to gear state help more towards real need and on encouraging more personal responsibility. They also accepted most of Labour's nationalization; only the steel industry was denationalized. Correspondingly, when Labour again obtained power in the sixties, it too accepted the mixed economy and the large private enterprise sector. (Indeed, some Labour leaders had even tried to get rid of the nationalization commitment from their party's constitution.) Though the Conservatives emphasized private responsibility and enterprise, and Labour stressed collectivism and state action, both operated within a consensus.

But this consensus was shattered in the seventies by union action to bring down a Tory government, a sharp move by Labour to the left, the infiltration of Marxists into the unions and into Labour's organization, and new trade union legislation which subordinated the liberty of the individual to the union machine. During the Callaghan government which was defeated in 1979, it became quite clear that the post-war consensus was dead, killed not by Margaret Thatcher but by the Labour left. There was no question of reviving it. In the 'winter of discontent' before the Conservative victory under Margaret Thatcher, the nation appeared to be on the brink of social breakdown. It was clear that Britain either had to go on to more full-blooded Socialism, or it had to retrace its thinking to 1945 and try to make a new start. It was now the business of the Conservative government to convince the people that a new start was both essential and possible.

In the speeches reprinted here, Mrs Thatcher defines the principles by which she would rebuild Britain and strengthen Britain's role in the world at large. That role had inevitably been diminished by the economic problems accentuated by the collapse of the post-war consensus. So economic recovery and the re-establishment of Britain's influence in the world at large had to proceed hand in hand. Under Labour from 1974 to 1979 Britain's position in foreign affairs declined perilously. The substantial left-wing minority in Mr Callaghan's Cabinet made it impossible for him to make a success of our membership of the European Community. Our partners looked to Britain for leadership, and they were constantly rebuffed.

Furthermore, massive cuts in defence spending, announced in 1975, undermined our contribution to Western defence. Consequently, Labour was unable to stand up firmly for Western interests in the face of growing Soviet aggression.

It was therefore against a sombre background that Mrs Thatcher spelt out her policies for the recovery of Britain.

COMMENTARY

*In April 1976 James Callaghan was elected leader of the
Labour Party, and that summer it became clear that a political
and economic storm was brewing which was likely to be worse
than any since that which had destroyed the Labour government of 1931 – though this time the enemy was inflation rather
than deflation. The long years of political juggling through
which Harold Wilson had kept his party together were over.*

*Once again, Labour was faced with a crisis of public spend-
ing. Since March 1974 the Wilson government had tried to
purchase union co-operation over wages by conceding the
social spending which the unions had demanded. Meanwhile,
Labour was pursuing its obsession with public ownership by
proceeding with shipbuilding and aircraft nationalization. Mr
Callaghan and his more responsible colleagues were brought
up against the fact that to avoid an economic crash, public
spending cuts had to be real – despite the resistance of his party
and the fact that a new post-war record of unemployment was
reached that summer. In July the then Chancellor Mr Denis
Healey had announced a package of £1000 million cuts, a
long-leaked figure which could not be retreated from without
a collapse of overseas confidence. It failed to halt the slide, and
on 29 September the government applied to the International
Monetary Fund for the largest ever loan in the Fund's history.*

Such was the end of Labour's so-called 'social contract' with the unions by which government spending was to have been counterbalanced by pay restraint to avoid inflation. When the Labour Party Conference assembled at the end of September 1976 the Callaghan government faced unprecedented attack from its followers, and was humiliatingly defeated on its spending cuts. The rhetoric of the conference was that everything that had happened was capitalism's fault and failure, and that it was not the business of a Labour government to maintain the capitalist economy. Mr Denis Healey was booed angrily during the short five-minute speech he was allowed (not being a member of the National Executive Committee) from below the platform. At the same time, the left was beginning its campaign to change the organization of the Labour Party and to enable constituency caucuses to deselect MPs as a way of expelling moderates, and to force Labour MPs to share with the more leftist constituencies and unions their right to elect the party leader. In the Labour Party the campaign for party democracy (that is to say, the supremacy of the party machine against parliamentary democracy) was now under way.

It was against a background of growing crisis that Margaret Thatcher, on 20 September, addressed the annual meeting of the Australian Liberal Party's federal council at Canberra, in the presence of the Australian Prime Minister, Mr Malcolm Fraser. Her speech was addressed to the underlying causes of the traumatic breakdown that had occurred in the former consensus. The clarity with which she had grasped the need for fundamental change was shown by her identification of the start of a 'new debate' in the Western world as a whole about the nature of democracy between those who 'consider they know what is good for people and those who think the people know best'. The themes of this speech, freedom and the individual, the relationship between private and public responsibility and the threat to liberty implicit in the nature of Socialism were those which were consistently to guide the actions of her future government.

Important though public action is for the well-being of the people, in the last analysis freedom is individual, and Mrs Thatcher's insistence that ultimately rights belong not to groups but to individuals is perhaps the most important single observation in the Canberra speech. But another of the thoughts she put to her audience was hardly less important: that we could lose our freedom imperceptibly and by stages as the proportion of the economy acquired by the state steadily came to overbalance the private sector. As it happened, less than a month after the speech at Canberra the Labour left-winger Judith Hart, speaking at the Labour Conference, uttered a single sentence (in arguing for bank nationalization) which exemplified the technique of the advancing left: 'Yester-day's extremism becomes tomorrow's moderation.' A basic theme of Mrs Thatcher's speeches was to get across to the people that there was nothing inevitable, predetermined or irreversible about the cleverly achieved ratchet process by which the whole political spectrum had been gradually shifted to the left in the post-war world.

The Liberal Party of Australia Federal Council

MELBOURNE, 20 SEPTEMBER 1976

In politics it is essential from time to time to raise one's eyes – as Winston Churchill said in one of his speeches – from the pages of economics and statistics, and look towards the broad sunlit uplands beyond. Today, I would like to try and do just that.

We face the last quarter of what by any standards is a fascinating century to live in, a century which has seen enormous scientific and technical change. Indeed, I doubt whether we shall ever again see so much change in such a short period: the whole of the communications and transport revolution, for example, cars, aeroplanes, telephones, radio, TV, the advances in medicine, automation in industry, and the immense output of labour-saving devices for the home. And most of this within the span of a single lifetime.

Political and social changes in the Western world have been just as far-reaching. The century has brought full adult suffrage: 'one person, one vote'; a vastly increased standard of living on a scale which has made yesterday's luxuries today's minimal necessities; and a range of educational opportunities so wide that it is sometimes difficult for the student to choose between them.

Against the background of technological, economic and social change, a new political debate has commenced in the

Western world. It is a debate about the nature and future of democracy. It is an encounter that concerns all free peoples.

It arises between the Socialists who consider they know best what is good for people, and those who think the people know best: between those who think a caring society is one in which everyone irrespective of need is provided with services from the government, and those who think it is one where people are given opportunity and encouragement to provide for themselves and their families, and where those in real need are given generous help.

You will argue that these issues are almost as old as the political debate itself, and that the arguments have been deployed since Aristotle first disagreed with Plato. Yes – but it is not the desire for an intellectual exercise but events themselves which have caused us to look afresh at where we are going, and see whether it is where we want to be.

We know from observation that in countries where the state owns everything, regulates everything, and directs and controls what people can do, political freedom is rapidly extinguished.

One of the most obvious changes in Western societies in recent years has been the great increase in the power of government at the expense of the citizen. The question is how much further can we go along this road and still remain a free and democratic society. Is it possible to lose our freedom, not by some dramatic change but slowly, almost imperceptibly, so that we hardly notice the change from day to day? If so, oughtn't we to turn back now before we reach the brink?

Let us then consider the role of government in modern-day society and see what we think it ought to be and what purpose it should serve.

I am reminded of an American saying: 'Any government that is big enough to give you all you want is strong enough to take away everything you have.' Much of our history in fact has been devoted to setting limits to the power of government, but the process has now been reversed.

Twenty years ago the private sector of the British economy

constituted 60 per cent of the National Product. It carried a public sector of 40 per cent. Those proportions have changed places. The state sector now forms 60 per cent of the GNP and the private sector 40 per cent.

As one of my colleagues said, 'In the mid-1950s the private horse was larger, stronger and heavier than its state jockey. Now the state jockey is half as big again as the horse.' No wonder the horse can't run very fast in the Economic Stakes.

We call ourselves a mixed economy; but the British mixed economy is more out of balance today than any other mixed economy in the West. Even some Socialists are saying that if the public sector gets much larger, democracy itself will be in danger. One consequence of this increasing role of government is that in Britain the citizen is suffering from one of the highest direct tax levels in the world. Our starting rate of income tax on earned income at 35 per cent is not merely the highest in Europe – it is actually the highest in the world according to one of our Treasury ministers. In addition only three countries in the world – Algeria, Egypt and Portugal – have a higher top marginal rate of income tax than our own of 83 per cent.

Like you, we not only look for reductions in the total of public expenditure, but we must make it our business to see that what is spent in our name is well spent.

We do not doubt the essential need for the government to take the lion's share of responsibility for the things that it can do best. Defence and law and order must clearly be in this category – although, ironically, these are the very services, defence in particular, that some Western Socialist governments seem least willing to maintain.

Among the other essential services, which only government can efficiently provide in an island like Britain, are most road and public utilities, and nearly all our schools, hospitals and social security insurance. Government also has a clear duty to help care for the sick and the old: to provide a safety net for all those who, through no fault of their own, fall into unemployment, poverty and deprivation.

It is no part of my party's thinking that we should dismantle the welfare state, any more than it is yours. Many of its most valuable benefits were introduced by Conservative governments, and I see you too have made a point of improving services where you think it is advisable, and increasing charges where justified. We must remember that nothing is free – or, as one phrase has it, 'There is no such thing as a free lunch.'

The real difference between the Conservative Party and our Socialist political opponents is that we believe the government should act to enlarge the freeedom of the individual to live his own life whilst they believe the government should diminish it. Our way upholds the importance of the individual and makes provision for him to develop his own talent. To us, all individuals are equally important, but all different. It is this difference which gives richness, variety and strength to the life of the community.

This philosophy is diametrically opposite to the Socialist approach which insists in putting everyone into efficient units to do whatever the collectivist Socialist wisdom considers best. But freedom is individual; there is no such thing as 'collective freedom'. Nevertheless a false 'collective' mystique has entered the language of Socialism.

Common to all collectivist theories is the presumption that 'social justice' is more equitable than justice to the individual; that the 'social wage' is more desirable than the income a man or woman earns, and spends or saves; that 'classes' matter more than people; above all that 'collective rights' are more important that the rights of the individual citizen. It is high time we exposed these fallacies.

Take the notion of 'collective rights' now ingrained into the vocabulary of Socialists. Of course, by joining together to do things collectively, we can and do acquire greater power. But we do not win greater rights.

The Socialist concept that rights belong 'collectively' to groups, and not to individuals, is extremely dangerous. It implies that some men, those in groups, are entitled to such rights, while others are not. If this sounds rather theoretical let me remind you how it can work out in practice.

The most conspicuous example is the Soviet Union. There,

more than anywhere else, the collectivist dogma has – in the name of 'the people' – made the state the owner and manager of all the means of production, distribution and exchange. All rights in Russia are 'collective rights'; all justice is 'social justice'; all assets are 'public assets'; even morality is judged by reference to 'Socialist ethics', 'state crimes', 'Marxist–Leninist principles'.

And the result? What began as a collectivist ideal degenerated swiftly into tyranny. 'Land and freedom' is what the peasants were promised. Lenin and Stalin is what they got. The dream of a people's state abolishing poverty, establishing peace, promoting the brotherhood of man, turned into a nightmare.

Far from abolishing poverty, Socialism has kept the vast majority of the Soviet people miles behind the Western world in standards of living and quality of life. Instead of 'superior productivity', based on worker control, its state-owned industries and collectivized farms are steadily falling further and further behind those of the West. Indeed, it was reported in March 1975 that 27 per cent of the total value of Soviet farm output comes from private plots that occupy less than 1 per cent of the nation's agricultural lands. At that rate, private plots are roughly forty times as efficient as land worked collectively.

Beyond these material comparisons is the spiritual measure of collectivism's failures in Russia. Socialist 'liberation' has meant the extinction of even that modicum of liberty which the Russians were beginning to gain under the Tsars. Socialist 'realism' has meant that neither artists nor writers have been free to express their own ideas. Anything that conflicts with the collectivist mystique is feared, and is accordingly condemned, and banned. Ironically, the 'condemning' and the 'banning' are done in the name of 'the people'. Thus, the people's courts, the public prosecutors, the state-controlled industries are presented to us as organs of 'collective' democracy. But they have nothing in common with democracy as we in the free world know it. They are the creatures of a new dictatorship. The people's revolution becomes the tyranny of whichever group, or gang, wins the struggle for power.

But what, you may ask, is the relevance of Russian Socialism to the debate about the role of the state in the Western world? It is the relevance of degree – and of warning.

Fundamentally, the collective mystique which inspires the Socialist parties of much of Europe, including Britain, differs from that in the Soviet system more in degree than in kind.

Thousands of British people have recently lost their individual right to work unless they join a trade union. And in many cases they no longer choose which trade union to belong to: they must join one chosen for them, on pain of being dismissed, and without compensation. Where numerous private firms are freely competing for labour, this may not be decisive. But now that so large a proportion of our economy is in the hands of nationalized industries, dismissing an employee for refusing to join the monopoly union in a monopoly industry can – and sometimes does – mean that a man trained as a train driver, steel worker or telephone engineer will never again be able to work in his chosen trade.

Is this not a case of the collective right being exercised at the cost of extinguishing personal rights? A few brave souls have resisted. But for the moment they are trapped between the collectivist pressures of trade union leaders who would rather a man was sacked than that he should defy their demands for conformity, and a Socialist state which has taken away – in the sacred name of equality – any effective protection for the rights of the individual.

That great observer of society, de Tocqueville, was right when he wrote that: 'Democracy and Socialism have nothing in common but one word – equality. But notice the difference – while democracy seeks equality in liberty, Socialism seeks equality in restraint and servitude.'

Democracy – the word is used in all sorts of ways and its meaning has become distorted. So let us look at what it really means. It was Abraham Lincoln, in one of the finest speeches of all time, the Gettysburg Address, who gave us the truest definition of democracy: government of the people, by the people, for the people.

Note well, what this does not mean. It does not mean government of a section of the people, by a section of the people, for a section of the people. On the contrary, its aim is to ensure that no section or group predominates over any other. The interests of each and every group are equally entitled to consideration. No interest, no minority is to be discarded or forgotten. Nor is government's consideration to be limited to those who are represented by some trade association, union or action group. Most people don't belong to such organizations, but their rights are every bit as important as those who do.

Every adult has a vote to elect Parliament. Parliamentary democracy is thus the only institution in the nation that truly represents all the people. A belief in parliamentary democracy is incompatible with belief in the superior rights of any group, section or class over any other.

But parliamentary democracy will be meaningless unless those who are elected to take the decisions actually do so. Of course they must consult with all important organizations, have constant discussions and dialogues with the people, see that the issues are clearly put so that everyone may know the consequences of any particular course of action. But the decision: that rests with Parliament, and it must yield to no one – or democracy will die.

There is one other vital safeguard on which so many of our fundamental liberties are based – the rule of law. Without it there can be no freedom.

Some Socialists tend to talk about freedom as if it were just freedom for some to oppress or to exploit others. But that is not freedom; it is tyranny, and it is just such a tyranny that the law is there to prevent. The purpose of the law is to protect the weak against the strong.

We have seen that the increasing power of governments can lead to the extinction of freedom. Can we be certain that our ancient institutions of parliamentary democracy and the rule of law would prove sufficient to prevent that from happening to us?

Regretfully, the answer is no. By themselves, democratic

institutions are not enough to preserve democracy. Parliaments act by majorities, and majorities are not always right. Let me illustrate the point. If two people vote to take everything away from a third, the decision would be by a majority; but it would not be right. This is an extreme example, but there have been cases where majority legislation has been less than fair to some citizens.

Then, can the rule of law stop a parliamentary majority using that majority unjustly? Again, the answer is no. The courts would have no alternative but to administer any law that had been passed by Parliament.

It follows that freedom cannot be guaranteed by these institutions alone. Ultimately, its survival rests on an unwritten moral law, on our belief in certain natural human rights, and that no one should displace them. They are the rock upon which the institutions of Parliament and the rule of law are built. If the foundations crumble, everything built upon them will perish.

It is this underlying moral code which leads ordinary people to judge what is right and just. It is this code which impels Parliament to use its majority as a trust, and pass laws in accordance with our concepts of fairness and justice. It is this code that maintains the rule of law.

We are all responsible for upholding these values and standards; not only our national leaders, but citizens as well.

Freedom is our most precious possession. To defend it and maintain it is no passive task, but one that requires continuous vigilance and resolve. The broad sunlit uplands can only be reached, and kept, by the efforts of the many as well as the few.

Let it never be said that the dedication of those who love freedom is less than the determination of those who would destroy it.

COMMENTARY

Throughout the autumn and winter of 1976–7 the economic storm, far from abating in response to Labour's earlier spending cuts, grew more serious. In October interest rates went to 15 per cent and there was a further 'Budget' of spending cuts and tax increases just before Christmas. The fact that the IMF's loan was only granted in tentative instalments was hardly a gesture of international confidence in Britain's future under Labour management. Swollen state spending was at the root of a rapidly rising inflation, which by February 1977 was approaching 17 per cent.

In trying to contain this the Callaghan government had started to cut the money supply and public spending (for doing both of which it was later persistently to attack Margaret Thatcher's administration). But it had taught the financial world to believe that its pay policy was the crucial support of its economic policy, and organized pay restraint was now so threatened, particularly in the public sector, as to have lost all real credibility.

In the past, Labour had been able to secure a degree of co-operation over pay by conceding social spending demanded by the unions. It could no longer afford this price. Unconditional pay restraint was now required, and the unions were in no mood to concede it. To add to the Labour government's diffi-

culties, its small House of Commons majority had been eroded and it could no longer even rely on the disinclination of a fragmented Opposition to combine against it. Mr Callaghan therefore had recourse to his pact with the Liberals in March 1977 to enable his party to postpone the time when it had to go to the country.

Such was the background to Margaret Thatcher's address to the Zurich Economic Society in March 1977, in which she discussed the way in which Britain had developed since the war, and rightly predicted a 'fundamental change in direction'. The tide was turning against collectivism and statism. In this speech she developed the themes of Canberra and perhaps most significantly the emphasis on the moral dimension – her insistence on the superiority of the Western non-Socialist system because it starts with the individual, his uniqueness and his responsibility.

This moral emphasis was important because for so long Labour and Socialism had claimed a kind of moral initiative; 'progressive' and 'Socialist' were almost synonyms. But a deep sense of disillusion with the post-war quasi-Socialist dispensation had set in and there was now a growing sense that old preconceptions had to be abandoned. Margaret Thatcher articulated the new thinking and understanding. The dominant thinking of the previous thirty-five years had ceased to carry conviction. There was proof of this in the fact that in its dying phase the Callaghan government was obliged (in order to avoid the Socialist siege economy which its leader and his close colleagues implictly recognized as inimical to freedom) to have recourse to remedies so antipathetic to its own party. The influence of such bodies as the Institute of Economic Affairs was a sign of a basic change in the intellectual climate, while the apologists for collectivism, and indeed for many of the other social fashions of the Establishment in the sixties and seventies, seemed increasingly to speak with a lack of inner conviction.

No politician achieves very much in the long run except by conviction. The Zurich speech was a notably complete and coherent statement of Margaret Thatcher's moral philosophy.

So convinced was she in the victory of her cause that she did not hesitate to express her hope that we should soon be witnessing the 'withering away' of the class struggle. That, it was clear, was also increasingly the hope of the mass of the British people. But in addressing this intellectually significant speech to a foreign audience, Mrs Thatcher was also making clear her belief that the problems faced by Britain were relevant to the world as a whole. There was a clear inference that the turning of the tide of thinking in Britain was a sign of hope to the Western world more generally.

The Zurich
Economic Society

ZURICH, 14 MARCH 1977

You have honoured me by your invitation as a practising politician, not an economist or financier. So I shall not attempt to instruct this highly expert and experienced gathering in economic affairs. Nor would you wish me to come all this way to describe the current situation in Britain, because I could tell you little more than you already know.

What I can offer you of interest is a perspective on the way Britain has developed in the post-war period, and my view of the fundamental change in direction which I believe is about to occur.

Though each country has its own special problems, successes and failures, by and large a similar evolution has taken place, and though I think we in Europe shall sink or swim together – we shall swim only if we will it.

So although I shall draw my examples from Britain, about which I can speak with more direct knowledge, the trend to which I refer goes well beyond our shores.

Had I spoken to you last year, I should have expressed faith in our nation and civilization, and its capacity for survival. But today I can offer you much more than faith; I bring you optimism rooted in present-day experience. I have reason to believe that the tide is beginning to turn against collectivism, Socialism, statism, dirigism, whatever you call it. And this turn is rooted in a revulsion against the sour fruit of Socialist experience. It is becoming increasingly obvious to many people who were intellectual Socialists that Socialism has failed to fulfil its promises, both in its more extreme forms in the Communist world, and in its compromise versions.

The tide flows away from failure. But it will not automatically float us to our desired destination. There have been tides before which were not taken, opportunities which were lost, turning points which came and went.

I do not believe that history is writ clear and unchallengeable. History is made by people: its movement depends on small currents as well as great tides, on ideas, perceptions, will and courage, the ability to sense a trend, the will to act on understanding and intuition. It is up to us to give intellectual content and political direction to those new dissatisfactions with Socialism in practice, with its material and moral failures, to convert disillusion into understanding.

If we fail, the tide will be lost. But if the opportunity is taken, the last quarter of our century can initiate a new renaissance matching anything in our island's long and outstanding history.

I know that many of you in continental Europe are gloomy about the economic and political condition of the United Kingdom. But I would remind you of the saying: 'The darkest hour is just before the dawn.'

I come to you in a mood of optimism, and I base it on two changes which I believe are taking place: a change in ideology, that is to say, in people's beliefs and attitudes; and a change in economic circumstances.

For forty years now, the 'progressive' — the up-to-the-moment — thing in Britain has been to believe in the virtues of collectivism. Ever since the 1930s, the intellectual left of British politics has looked through rose-tinted spectacles at the real or imagined successes of planned economies, like those in Eastern Europe. Even Mr Callaghan, for example — not conspicuously a member of the intellectual left — said as recently as 1960: 'I have not the slightest doubt that the economic measures and the Socialist measures, which one will find in the countries of Eastern Europe, will become increasingly powerful against the unco-ordinated planless society in which the West is living at present.' This view has been carrying increasing weight in the Labour Party.

It is true that in what they have said, senior Socialist politicians have continued to affirm their faith in the mixed economy. But in the mixed economy, as in a cocktail, it is the mix that counts. In their favoured mix, collectivism has taken an ever larger proportion. The words of these politicians expressed a belief that private enterprise had a major role to play in the economy. But their deeds extended government into almost every part of business life. The 'progressives' had their way.

The nationalized sector of the economy has been extended far beyond the major industries of fuel, transport and steel. In the next few weeks the aircraft and shipbuilding industries will be nationalized; whilst the Labour Party's programme for the future, published last year, includes plans for taking over banks and insurance companies.

Private firms in difficulties have been taken into public ownership. More and more of the taxpayer's money has been pumped into companies that no prudent banker could go on supporting for long, because instead of creating wealth, they use up wealth created by others.

The state sector has come to dominate the mixed economy. Its insatiable demand for finance has inhibited the operation of the market sector. Yet the public sector can only live on private enterprise, on whose surplus it relies.

This is where we now stand. But I believe that we have come to the end of the trend. There is a growing realization in Britain that the 'progressives' were wrong. They are being proved wrong by the failure of the very system they advocated. To finance the extension of Socialism on so vast a scale, taxation has risen to penal levels. We have all seen the results – for living standards, for incentive and for enterprise – of the excessive tax burden in Britain.

Yet even these unacceptable levels of taxation have not been enough to finance the public sector. The government has been borrowing vast sums of money, both within Britain and overseas. But even these borrowings were not enough. The government turned to printing money in order to finance a public sector deficit that neither taxpayers nor lenders would finance in full. With a huge rise in the money supply, hyper-inflation became a real threat: and that threat does not end with economics. When money can no longer be trusted, it is not only the economic basis of society that is undermined, but its moral basis too. (I shall return to that part of the argument later.) And when the economic foundations are undermined, those who suffer most are the ordinary working people, the very people in whose name the Socialists claim to be acting.

For it is our system, the free enterprise system, which delivers the goods to the great mass of the people. We may have been remiss in not saying this with sufficient vigour in the past; well, I shall not be remiss this evening.

For it is not only in my country that Socialism has failed the nation. It is well known that the ultimate aim of every Soviet planner is for his country to equal the levels of production in the USA. It is the West, not the East, which sells off surpluses of grain and other foodstuffs to the planned economies, and also gives them to the countries of the Third World.

It is Western technology which the East seeks to acquire. And it is the Western world, those countries with essentially capitalist economies, from which the British government has recently sought, and received, help for the pound.

The Socialist countries do not attempt to conceal their admiration for the productive achievements of the free economy. But what they do argue is that the avalanche of goods which the capitalist system produces is available only for the well-to-do. This is totally false. It misconceives the very essence of capitalist achievement. As Josef Schumpeter put it: 'The capitalist engine is first and last an engine of mass production, which unavoidably means also production for the masses ... It is the cheap cloth, the cheap fabric, boots, motor cars and so on that are the typical achievements of capitalist production and not as a rule improvements that would mean

24

much to the rich man.' In brief, the material superiority of the free society gives its main benefits to the very people the Socialists claim to cherish.

Continuing benefits depend upon innovation. It is innovation which lies at the heart of economic progress, and only the free economy can provide the conditions in which it will flourish.

Alfred Marshall, doyen of nineteenth-century British economists, said the capitalist economy frees constructive genius 'to work its way to the light and to prove its existence by attempting difficult tasks on its own responsibility, and succeeding in them: for those who have done most for the world have seldom been those whom their neighbours would have picked out as likely for the work.' How much more will the remote, central planner fail to pick the winner?

This inability to foresee from the centre where the next innovation will come is a key failing of the planned economy.

Collectivists may flatter themselves that wise men at the centre – with whom they identify – can make better decisions, and waste fewer resources than a myriad of individual decision-makers and independent organizations all over the country.

Events in Britain have shown that, wise or not, those at the centre lack the knowledge, foresight and imagination required. They are overworked and overwhelmed. They are certainly surprised by events.

I have dwelt so far on the material superiority of the free society. But we must not focus our attention exclusively on the material, because, although important, it is not the main issue. The main issues are moral. In warfare, said Napoleon, the moral to the material is as three to one. You may think that in civil society the ratio is even greater.

The economic success of the Western world is a product of its moral philosophy and practice. The economic results are better because the moral philosophy is superior. It is superior because it starts with the individual, with his uniqueness, his responsibility, and his capacity to choose.

Surely this is infinitely preferable to the Socialist–statist philosophy which sets up a centralized economic system to which the individual must conform, which subjugates him, directs him and denies him the right to free choice. Choice is the essence of ethics: if there were no choice, there would be no ethics, no good, no evil; good and evil have meaning only in so far as man is free to choose.

In our philosophy the purpose of the life of the individual is not to be the servant of the state and its objectives, but to make the best of his talents and qualities. The sense of being self-reliant, of playing a role within the family, of owning one's own property, of paying one's way, are all part of the spiritual ballast which maintains responsible citizenship, and provides the solid foundation from which people look around to see what more they might do, for others and for themselves.

That is what we mean by a moral society; not a society where the state is responsible for everything, and no one is responsible for the state.

I said earlier that the better moral philosophy of the free society underlies its economic performance. In turn the material success of the free society enables people to show a degree of generosity to the less fortunate unmatched in any other society. It is noteworthy that the Victorian era – the heyday of free enterprise in Britain – was also the era of the rise of selflessness and benefaction.

The second reason why the free society is morally better is because it entails dispersal of power away from the centre to a multitude of smaller groups, and to individuals. On the other hand, the essence of collectivism is the concentration of power in large groups, and in the hands of the state at the centre: as Lord Acton reminded us, absolute power corrupts absolutely!

The left had traditionally argued that the dispersal of power, coupled with the freedom given to the individual, could, and did, lead to the power being unjustly used. But part of the price of freedom is that some will abuse it. And in free societies this problem is dealt with by a strong and impartial legal system designed to ensure justice between individuals, and to safeguard the weak against the strong. The evolution of such a system was an essential element in the growth of freedom. It is ironic that many intellectuals espoused the Socialist creed because they thought it would prevent the development of harmful monopoly power. They believed that their system would obviate it. They took it for granted that Socialism would protect the weak against the strong. They forgot that when the Socialists gained power they would become the strong, and would resist any check on their own power.

How shaken and disabused are many of these intellectuals today. And rightly so, for we are now facing the crisis of Socialism: economic failure, social and political tensions; a decline in freedom of choice in education, health, economic activity.

Experience has shown that Socialism corrodes the moral values which form part of a free society. Traditional values are also threatened by increasing state regulation. The more the state seeks to impose its authority, the less respect that authority receives. The more living standards are squeezed by taxation, the greater is the temptation to evade that taxation. The more pay and prices are controlled, the more those controls are avoided.

In short, where the state is too powerful, efficiency suffers and morality is threatened.

Britain in the last two or three years provides a case-study of why collectivism will not work. It shows that the 'progressive' theory was not progressive. On the contrary, it proved retrograde in practice. This is a lesson that democrats all over the world should heed.

Yet I face the future with optimism. Our ills are creating their own antibodies. Just as success generates problems, so failure breeds the will to fight back and the body politic strives to restore itself.

The ordinary Briton is neither political philosopher nor economist. He has no clearly articulated theory to tell him why the free society is superior to the collectivist one. But he has felt the shortcomings of collectivism and he senses that something is fundamentally wrong. This explains why many people are giving up their support for Socialist ideas and policies.

Nor is the reaction against Socialism confined to politics and ideology. It is also practical. Under our very eyes, new forms of free association, free economic activity, great and small, are being born, thanks to the resourcefulness of many men and women.

I am reminded of an observation by Adam Smith:

> The uniform, constant and uninterrupted effort of every man to better his condition, the principle from which public and national, as well as private, opulence is originally derived, is frequently powerful enough to maintain the natural progress of things toward improvement, in spite both of the extravagance of government and of the greatest errors of administration. Like the unknown principle of animal life, it frequently restores health and vigour to the constitution, in spite not only of the disease, but of the absurd prescriptions of the doctor.

The great mutual benefit activities, 'the people's capitalism', are burgeoning. Between them, occupational pension funds and life insurance own a good half of all quoted securities on behalf of their members. Thanks to them, and to other charities and non-profit-making activities which hold securities, it is estimated that 85 per cent of the population has an indirect, if not direct, share in British industry. The vast majority of the population is thus partcipating in capitalism.

The investors and the workers have become the same people. As shareholders and employees they have an identical interest in industrial and commercial prosperity.

We may soon be witnessing the withering away of the class struggle, to adapt a well-known phrase.

Then there are the building societies (which are mutual mortgage banks), which have enabled a good third of the population to buy their homes, lending and borrowing without subsidies or assistance, asking only to be allowed to get on with their jobs.

There is the phenomenon that however many resources are poured into the existing nationalized sector, its employment and share of production tend to fall, while private activities expand, when they have half the chance. The City of London responds to reduced scope for its activities on behalf of British industry (because industry's profits have been eroded) by expanding its services on behalf of the rest of the world. Our manufacturers expand overseas and in Europe, attracting local capital – using the initiative and capacity which, under present circumstances, are only partly used at home. That way they keep their management teams in being for the day when industry will be able to expand in Britain. And were it not for their repatriated earnings, our economic position would be worse.

The great North Sea oil adventure was initiated and financed entirely by free enterprise, without help from government. The oil companies overcame not only the unprecedented technological problem created by North Sea weather hazards, but also the political hazard posed by hostility to free enterprise and profit.

All these developments and potentialities illustrate the inherent vitality of our people. We need have no fear as we engage in the battle of ideas.

We have a ready audience. The younger generation may produce its wild men, but is also produces large numbers of young people for whom the post-war settlement has failed, and who are ready to examine our arguments on their merits. The opportunity is ours if we can grasp it instead of meeting the Socialists half-way.

Mr Chairman, when Winston Churchill spoke in this hall in September 1946, he called for an act of faith in re-creating the European family. It is an act of faith, too, which is required today by all of us in restoring the free society.

Not far from Winston Churchill's country home lived one of our best known national poets, Rudyard Kipling. He and Winston were great friends and mutual admirers. The new renaissance of which I spoke was perhaps best described by Kipling:

*So when the world is asleep, and there seems no hope of
 waking
Out of some long, bad dream that makes her mutter and
 moan,
Suddenly, all men arise to the noise of fetters breaking,
And everyone smiles at his neighbour and tells him his soul
 is his own.*

COMMENTARY

By the summer of 1977 the Callaghan government was still hanging on to office although it had lost part of its Budget strategy (it was defeated over petrol tax and even over part of its personal taxation proposals). Mr Callaghan had nevertheless announced that there would be no autumn election. Meanwhile the government had had to breach the constitutional convention of collective Cabinet responsibility by allowing dissident (anti-European Community) ministers to vote against the bill for direct elections to the European Parliament. This was the direct consequence of Sir Harold Wilson's licence to his ministers, when he was Prime Minister, to disagree over Europe. There remained a powerful anti-European Trojan horse in the Labour Cabinet. That was, perhaps, inevitable since the bulk of Labour activists were, as they remain, deeply anti-European and almost xenophobic towards Britain's partners in the Community.

The contrast between Labour on the one hand, and the Conservatives and Mrs Thatcher on the other, in their approach to the Community has persistently been stark. Mrs Thatcher has often been accused of being cold towards the Community because she dislikes its bureaucracy and its budgetary waste (particularly on producing unwanted farm commodities) and because after becoming Prime Minister she fought hard, without mincing words, to end the situation in which Britain was paying a wholly disproportionate share of the European Budget. But her speeches and her conduct over a long period both show this accusation to be false. Because she has never used the emollient, even sycophantic, language of the Brussels aficionados, because she did not adopt the oleaginous style of so many British Euro-fanatics who seem to think it coarse to argue forcibly in such cultivated circles, she was regularly called 'anti-European'.

In fact, Mrs Thatcher displayed very early an awareness of the political importance of Europe. In this speech to the Centro Italiona di Studi per la Conciliazione Internazionale at Rome she firmly places the European Community in its Western and Nato context (even though not all members of the EEC were full Nato members) as a bulwark against Soviet expansionism. Very convincingly, in view of the obstructive attitude of the Labour Party towards European Parliamentary elections, she staked the Conservatives' claim to be 'the European Party' of Britain, and advocated a drawing together internationally of the parties of the centre and right (despite obstacles of nomenclature), which lacked the international links with their equivalents comparable to those of the Socialist parties.

It is especially significant that even at this stage she focused on the growing practice among European Foreign Offices of pooling information instead of jealously keeping it to themselves, and it is, of course, precisely the pragmatic growth of such links (rather than formal acts of union) which has made European co-operation an increasing reality since then. She rightly stressed that Europe's views would be lost if Europe spoke with many voices, leaving only Washington and Moscow to be heard. Coming from such a staunch supporter of the priority of the British–American alliance, that position is all the more important, and it is a statement that has needed to be made from time to time, not least because Washington sometimes gives the impression of preferring that the European nations should talk to it severally with weaker voices.

The Centro Italiano di Studi per la Conciliazione Internazionale

ROME, 24 JUNE 1977

It is exactly thirty years since your Centre began its work. I venture to suggest that never during this period has it been more important than now to exchange views and to learn more of the principles and purposes which have in different ways brought us all into public life. That, as I understand, is the purpose of the Centre.

No true European can fail to love Italy. Your country is the birthplace of so much of our common civilization; of the abiding Roman concepts of law and self-discipline; of the universal Catholic tradition; of the glories of the Renaissance, its paintings and sculptures and buildings; of the Roman opera and the music of La Scala, Milan.

But not only do we love and admire the civilization of Rome. We need you as allies. Italy is one of the keys to the defences of the Western world in the Mediterranean, and we count on your support to sustain them. Your country and its leaders also provided much of the impetus towards the creation of the European Community. It is fitting that its constitution bears the title of the Treaty of Rome.

The British and the Italians have been friends for a very long time. Rome indeed was one of our most famous and successful invaders! Today, we share many problems: inflation, indebtedness, falling living standards. But we also share common aspirations, a common love of freedom, a common preference for democracy – above all, a common belief in the value, the spiritual value, of individual human beings.

It is these common values that I speak of today. For it is they which lie at the heart of my vision of Europe, and it is on them that my party – and, I believe, the vast majority of my fellow countrymen – are determined to build for the future.

The European Community is twenty-one years old this year. Twenty-one years is not a long time in the history of Europe. But today, as in 1956, Europe is confronted by threats from without and within.

The threat from without comes largely from the armed might and expansionist aims of the Soviet Union. That is why all those who hold freedom dear as yet have no safe alternative but to maintain our defences, within the Nato alliance.

My party, when we return to office, is totally committed to this. By the same token we are pledged to seek a lasting peace. It is in this context that I approach the Belgrade Conference at which the 35 signatory nations of the Helsinki Agreement will be able to assess how much progress has been made in putting into practice the clauses on security, economic relations and human rights.

The Helsinki Agreement was intended to be treated as a whole. Nations cannot expect to choose only those parts which they prefer and ignore the rest. So it is no good talking about trade, while forgetting about security; no use promoting exchanges of films and ballets, while ignoring human rights.

As far as security is concerned, we seek no confrontation with the Soviet Union or with any Communist government. Peace is our purpose. Keeping it is my profession. But there can be no peace without security, any more than there can be liberty without order. We are therefore entitled to seek at Belgrade, and beyond, far more tangible evidence than so far has emerged that the Soviets are prepared to match the Western world's aim to turn down the rising graph of both conventional and nuclear armaments.

The Helsinki Agreement also provides for co-operation in the fields of economics, science and technology. I have no doubt this is of particular concern to the Soviet Union. Trade with Eastern Europe can indeed bring mutual benefits. But it has to be on terms which ensure that the benefits are fairly shared by both sides. We must beware that the competition that naturally exists between free countries does not lead us to give benefits to the Soviet Union which help it harm our interests.

Our trade and financial relations with the Eastern bloc must therefore form part of a coherent design, rooted in principles of freedom. We must try to make it easier for the countries of Eastern Europe to choose their own policies and their own trading partners in accordance with the wishes of their own people. We have a role here which the United States with all its strength and eloquence cannot perform, a role which belongs to us because we are Europeans, a role which the Community should heed.

Of all the clauses of Helsinki, the European Community has a particular interest in those which contain the solemn declaration of all signatory governments to uphold and extend liberty.

It was largely at our insistence that these undertakings were included. And we do not ask more than we grant. Communist ideas circulate freely in the West: for us freedom is as natural as the air we breathe.

Where there is no free press, no free speech, no independent judiciary, no respect for the rule of law, there can be no safeguard against tyranny, and no brake on those who may be tempted to use force to achieve their ends.

I welcome President Carter's renewed emphasis on human rights. It has put the moral commitment back into the forefront of politics. We Europeans should not hesitate to range ourselves along with our American partners in standing up for human rights, wherever they are in question. Are we not free peoples, choosing our own governments, respecting one another's rights as individuals under the law? And are not those who live under Soviet Communism denied both rights and freedom as we in the West understand them?

Ours is a free partnership. Theirs is a forced partnership. It is not in their interest, or ours, that this contrast should be blurred or disguised.

Our first duty to liberty is to keep our own. But it is also our duty – as Europeans – to keep alive in the Eastern as well as the Western half of our Continent those ideas of human dignity which Europe gave to the world.

Let us therefore resolve to keep the lamps of freedom burning bright so that all who look to the West from the shadows of the East need not doubt that we remain true to those human and spiritual values that lie at the heart of European civilization.

To perform this role the Community needs to strengthen itself. For we face dangers from within as well as from without. Dangers of disunity, and of disillusion. Some people are beginning to have doubts about the European idea in practice. At home there are those, some of them politicians, who blame the Community for all our problems. Others, a small but vociferous minority, would have Great Britain pull out.

That is not the position of the party I lead. We are the European party in the British Parliament and among the British people; and we want to co-operate wholeheartedly with our partners in this joint venture.

The Conservative Government of which I was a member in 1961–64 first tried to negotiate British entry into the Community under the leadership of Mr Harold Macmillan. The goal was not achieved until 1972 under Mr Heath. Mr John Davies, who sits with me here today, played a major and skilful part in the arrangements for British entry, and now speaks for the Conservative Party on European, Commonwealth and foreign affairs. We negotiated entry on the only possible basis – namely that we accepted the basic rules and arrangements which the Community had already made, subject to transitional provisions. But we made it clear that once we were members we would work to persuade our partners that some policies needed to be adjusted to take account of our entry.

This is the way the Community works. Its policies are not sacred or static. They evolve year by year as the needs of its members change.

This is particularly true of the common agricultural policy. Some people in Britain place all the blame for higher food prices on the CAP. They simply have not studied the facts. The most striking increases endured by the British housewife have been in foods not covered by the CAP at all; for example, tea and coffee. We can attribute the blame for these increases to the weather, the growth of international demand and the decline in the value of the pound sterling. It is superficial and absurd to blame them on Europe.

Nevertheless it is fair to point out that the CAP has been administered in a way which has produced some damaging results. The price review this year was somewhat more realistic; it provided for a modest general increase in prices, at a rate considerably lower than the increase in farmers' costs.

But in general the Ministers of Agriculture have fixed prices at a level which are likely to produce embarrassing surpluses. Too high a proportion of the Community's budget has gone in guaranteeing these prices, too little in making it easier for the farmer whose costs are high to find a better livelihood in another way. The problem has been made worse by the widening gap between strong and weak currencies within the Community. The Community has had to spend valuable time and resources juggling with incredibly complicated compensation arrangements, to no one's satisfaction. The effect in Britain has been particularly ironic. On the one hand the Community has had to spend up to £1 million a day protecting the British consumer from the failure of the British government to protect the pound. On the other hand the British farmer, as a highly efficient producer, has so far been deprived by his own government of the advantage which he had every reason to expect.

The reform of the CAP is therefore a major objective of any British government. It is also a major interest of the whole Community, as the Commission has recognized.

The aim of this reform as I see it must be to fix prices each year at a level which will encourage the efficient producer and discourage the inefficient. Such a reform will not be achieved by loud words or sharp tactics, but by striking a better balance between the producer and consumer in each price review. This will be a complicated effort requiring much patience. But I believe it can succeed because we shall be working with the trend and not against it. We shall be helping the progress towards a more efficient and competitive European agriculture which has been under way for several years.

One reason why I am confident that we can put our house in order on agriculture is that the Community has already achieved so much in other fields, particularly in international trade. Further, its member nations have achieved some success in working out common positions for the Community to take towards the outside world.

It happened in Paris during the North–South dialogue. It happened at Helsinki and I hope it will be repeated at the Belgrade Conference this year.

In the old days, the diplomats of different European countries used to guard their secrets jealously as if they were proofs of success. Nowadays our Foreign Offices increasingly are pooling their information.

But more is needed. The joint declarations issued by foreign ministers and heads of government certainly have their significance, but what really matters is joint effort to translate words into deeds.

There are many great issues that affect us: supplies of Middle East oil, the advance of the Soviet fleet, the security of Africa. If Europe speaks with many voices her views will be lost. Only the dialogue between Washington and Moscow will be heard.

Let us therefore take back from the Americans the motto they borrowed from you: '*E pluribus unum*'. Inevitably from time to time there will be differences of emphasis and even clashes of interest between member countries. But compared with the interests we have in common, the differences which divide us shrink into insignificance. They must not be allowed to rob us of the prize which could be won by more effective common action – a new upsurge of European vitality, a European *risorgimento*.

It is a characteristic of our civilization that the ideas which tend to influence its people most profoundly are not laid down by governments. The tides of debate ebb and flow, adapting policies and changing attitudes. Increasingly I find that the debates in each country are coming to resemble one another. More and more of the issues which we tackle now have a European and sometimes a world dimension. Less and less is it possible for any of our governments to succeed if they try to tackle their problems in isolation.

I do not believe that the nation-states in Europe will wither away. I do believe that those who take part in the political life of the nation-states need to work much more closely than they have done hitherto with like-minded colleagues in other countries.

We see the need for this in the approach to Direct Elections to the European Parliament. This is an obligation to which all member countries are committed, and for our part we in the Conservative Party intend to honour it. Anyone with a sense of history must recognize as a remarkable advance the prospect that in a single election, nine European countries will go to the polls to elect representatives to a single democratic assembly. This step forward makes it necessary, if only out of self-interest, for political leaders to come together with others whose support and friendship they will increasingly need.

There is a danger that in this process the Socialist side of the argument will have an advantage, because for more than half a century machinery has existed for co-operation between Socialist parties. Co-operation between Communist parties can still be regarded as a matter of course.

By contrast, parties of the centre and right have been separate and fragmented. We see this fragmentation in the present nominated European Parliament where there are no less than four political groups representing the centre and right.

In saying this I am of course well aware of the remarkable progress made since the war by the Christian Democrat parties in Europe. They have produced great statesmen, not least in Italy, who played a major part in laying the foundations of the European Community. It must be good news for Europe that the Christian Democrat parties have increasingly come together and that they have recently formed a single 'European People's Party' within the Community.

Nevertheless it is right to point out that in two of the member states of the Community, Britain and Denmark, there are no Christian Democrat parties and that in France the Centre Democrats are relatively small. A wider basis of co-operation is therefore necessary if we are to further our cause against those who hold political views of a kind which we of the centre and right instinctively reject.

Of course I understand that the tactical situation varies in each country, and that it is often thought advisable for parties of the centre and right to co-operate with democratic socialists. Political parties must be free to make their own choices in this kind of situation.

But equally if we look on Europe as a whole, it is clear that the present fragmentation of the centre and right gives to the left an advantage which the rest of us cannot afford. I am delighted that there is now a much closer co-operation inside the present European Parliament between the Christian Democrat and Conservative Groups.

But I am also sure that something wider is necessary. As a first step we need to co-operate in practical matters connected with the Direct Elections campaign. I hope that this co-operation can lead after Direct Elections to a clearer and firmer alliance between the parties of the centre and right.

Of course, I realize that there are obstacles we have to over-come. One of them is a name. The party which I lead in Britain has for more than a century been called the Conservative Party. Throughout that time there have been arguments whether or not this is the right name. We have grown used to it, but I am fully aware that when translated into other lan-guages, the word Conservative acquires completely different overtones. In Italian, for example, it is a term of criticism. It has certainly been a hindrance to co-operation between like-minded parties.

I would ask those who shy away from the word to concen-trate their attention on the common ground which exists between the British Conservative Party and the Christian

Democrats and other centre right parties in Europe.

As our contacts with these parties multiply, the extent of this common ground becomes more impressive. I have found this on my own visits since 1975 to France, Germany, Holland, and now to Italy.

The British Conservative Party does not cling to yesterday. It adapts the best of yesterday to provide for the needs of tomorrow. We are proud of our heritage and because we are proud of it we wish to add to it. One of our greatest political thinkers, Edmund Burke, expressed our philosophy in these words: 'People will not look forward to posterity, who never look backward to their ancestors.'

We believe in political freedom as providing the only framework within which men and women can live lives worthy of their talents and of their human dignity. This is also the basis of the European Community. As the countries applying to join know, membership is only possible for those who accept true democracy as the foundation of their political life. I cannot conceive that any country could continue as a member of the Community if it allowed within its own frontiers an irreversible shift to totalitarian practices, whether of left or right. The European Community can have no room for part-time democrats.

We also believe in economic freedom, because the evidence shows that a free economic system provides the individual and the community with the best hope of that material prosperity which is the legitimate aim of our peoples.

But when we speak of political and economic freedom we do not mean freedom to ignore the rights of others, or freedom to amass wealth without any regard for its use.

We accept the moral commitments of a free society, which have been handed down to us from their origins among the Jews and Greeks through the rich development of the Christian tradition. There is a commitment to respect for the law. There is a commitment to the family as the natural and fundamental unit of society. There is a commitment to high standards of integrity in education. It is significant that in country after country of Europe, including my own, education is coming to the fore as a political issue. There is a commitment to the widest possible diffusion of ownership. Finally, there is a commitment to help the weak and the unfortunate. Indeed only a free society can create the resources adequate to care for those in need.

These are commitments which we Conservatives have spelt out in our most recent statement of policy, 'The Right Approach'. They are commitments which we share with every Christian Democrat party. They are fundamental beliefs which we need to proclaim often and together.

We should not be concerned only with protecting those values in our own nations, or in our own European Community. Liberty is worth defending – but it is equally worth exporting. So where human rights are concerned, all true Europeans are evangelists. The story of our Continent is of European man, the explorer and the trader, the missionary and the settler, carrying the fruits of his scientific discoveries, of his artistic and cultural achievements, above all of his political values, across every sea and continent.

No European need apologize for the accomplishments of our peoples in the wider world. Nor did the process stop with the coming of age of the United States of America, the republics of Latin America and the former British dominions of Canada, Australia and New Zealand.

The time has not yet come – I hope it never will – when the European Community turns inward upon itself. For Europe is the source of history's greatest endeavour, whereby the spirit of man, restless and ever ambitious, seeks always to renew itself by reaching outwards and upwards.

The challenge for the next generation is to use the growing authority that will come from the greater unity of Europe to span the gaps between races and continents, between the rich and the poor, between the free and the unfree of the world.

This is a great work, and it cannot be carried out by timid minds. We must embark on these honourable causes with a sure hope and trust in ourselves. We must tirelessly assert the truth of the free society, and we must match its opportunities with our courage. If not us, who? If not now, when?

COMMENTARY

In her Brussels address, Margaret Thatcher firmly placed the European Community as a major element in the defence of democracy and the West. The speech was made at a time when the Community was intensely unpopular, being seen as a body which caused the British to pay more than they need for their food, which was responsible for butter mountains sold cheaply to Russia, and which was prone to irritating bureaucratic interference. Mrs Thatcher herself acknowledged this last point, with a reference to the hindrance to unity caused by hundreds of 'petty regulations', but her basic concern was the Community's political importance.

At this time the Community was discussing the possibility of enlargement by the admission of Greece, Spain and Portugal. For some British anti-Marketeers, enlargement was welcomed on the grounds that it would weaken the supranational pretensions of the EEC. Their hope was that it would become so unwieldy, disparate and heterogeneous that it might turn into no more than a loose free trade area which would not disturb our sovereignty with supranational interference. But, of course, the purpose of admitting the additional countries was not to weaken the political significance of the Community but to strengthen it. Enlargement was designed to promote the social and political stability of Europe's potentially weak

Mediterranean flank. The essential purpose was the preservation of democracy in Greece, Spain and Portugal, and safeguarding the nations against Communism by admitting them to the prosperity of the Community. In this respect the theme of Mrs Thatcher's Brussels address was in accord with Brussels thinking, sceptical though she was known to be about such ideas as a supranational political authority and a European currency, both of which were being deployed at the time. The Brussels speech was remarkably prescient in encouraging reflection on the kind of Europe to be aimed at. Perhaps the most significant aspect of this was Mrs Thatcher's willingness to consider a defence role for Europe, and her reminder that while both Nato and the Community had their headquarters in Brussels, and 'both were concerned with the protection and prosperity of Western Europe', they had 'little to say to one another'.

'Can this be right?' she asked. At the time this part of Mrs Thatcher's speech aroused a degree of scorn among some Euro-enthusiasts who put their trust in Brussels institution-building. They said she didn't understand that defence, in the Nato sense, was in no way the Community's business, and that she ignored the fact that membership of the two was not identical though overlapping. That reaction showed how little they understood her grasp of the indivisibility of foreign and defence policy, and the extent to which the ordinary day-to-day working of ministers and officials of the member states would inevitably breed a degree of practical European political co-operation which would increasingly make a 'European political voice' a reality – and this would inevitably become relevant to Nato's business. The European states will not draw together by constitution-building but by the pragmatic cultivation of unity. That was the approach to which Margaret Thatcher has repeatedly tried to convert her European partners since she became Prime Minister.

Les Grandes Conférences Catholiques

BRUSSELS, 23 JUNE 1978

It is an honour as well as a great pleasure to follow today the many people of distinction who have spoken in this series of lectures. The tradition of Christian thought which you uphold has decisively influenced my own political thinking and that of my party. It has helped to shape the Europe to which we all belong. It is an essential sinew of our foreign policy in the Western world.

We in Britain watched with anxiety the invasion of Shaba. We understood that our anxiety was as nothing compared with the anxiety here in Belgium. We admired the speed and success with which the French and Belgian forces carried out their mission.

But the events in Zaire also served as one of the many warnings that both the analysis and the policies of the West may sometimes be defective. We must see how to reshape our policies to meet the needs of a changing situation.

We were caught by surprise. The invasion of Shaba and the savagery and destructiveness which accompanied it form part of a pattern which we had not anticipated. We lack a common policy towards Zaire and other countries threatened by the Soviet scramble for Africa.

But this in turn depends on our total view of world affairs and Europe's part in them.

Let me begin with the principles which guide our approach to foreign affairs, then consider in turn the promising signs and the worrying signs, before coming on to a number of key issues and policies.

One of the difficulties about foreign affairs is the gap between the bland, unexceptionable but platitudinous statements usually enunciated when principles are called for, and the immense complexity, and hasty improvisation, with which policy is usually carried out.

The difficulty is not new. A nineteenth-century Conservative Prime Minister, Lord Salisbury, one of the best we have ever had, when asked to define his policy could go no further than say that, so far as he knew, British foreign policy was 'to float lazily downstream putting out a diplomatic boathook to avoid collision' when necessary.

That definition hardly did justice to the subtlety and wisdom of the actual policy of Salisbury. But in the nineteenth century, matters of foreign policy, though complicated, at least did not have to be worked out under the shadow of nuclear arms. A modern Prime Minister in Europe can hardly avoid realizing that the decisions to which he may have to be a party will be far harder than those taken by statesmen at any previous time.

My first principle is that as long as we have potential enemies, we must recognize that peace can only be maintained through strength. Our first duty to freedom is to defend our own. Foreign policy and defence policy must be interlocked, the first dictating the second.

There is no case whatsoever, as has happened too often in history, for military men to dictate diplomacy. There must be political control. At the same time, foreign policy must be supported by adequate military strength and understanding.

We are concerned to defend not only our sovereignty and that of our allies, but the way of life which enhances that sovereignty's value. In that context, and this is my second point, we have to distinguish between the 30 or so sovereign states in the world which are democracies and the 120 or so which are not.

It is true that none of our democracies is perfect. Most of our time and effort as democratic politicians is spent on trying to improve them. But we have nothing to apologize for when dealing with the despotisms which seem to threaten us in Europe and elsewhere.

Here in the Western community of democratic nations, war between us has been renounced as an instrument of foreign policy. Not so the Communist states. Democracies in the twentieth century have never been engaged against each other in warfare in any major way. To reduce the risk of war, therefore, we must work for steady progress towards more democracies. With the advancing tide of democracy, the risk of war recedes. If the tide of democracy recedes, the risk of war advances.

Of course, we have to have relations with a great many countries which are not democracies. Our antipathy to Communism will not diminish our efforts to reach whatever understanding we can with Russia and other Communist states. It would be naive to suppose that many African states will move very far, very quickly towards democratic government, but that is no reason for slackening our endeavours to help them achieve the prosperity and quality of life needed to underpin national political stability. But we should never hesitate to proclaim that democracies are morally superior to all states which are subject to tyrannical governments.

The third principle is that foreign policy commitments are not to be made and unmade at will. We are bound by past commitments. We have a respect for past contracts, both as governments and as ordinary citizens. We cannot expect others to keep their word to us unless we keep our word to them. When Chancellor Bethman Hollweg of Imperial Germany tore up the guarantee of Belgium's neutrality in 1914, dismissing it as a scrap of paper, he was tearing up something far more important than he seems to have known.

Continuity does not of course stop the evolution of policy nor the proper renegotiation of commitments in the light of changing circumstances.

Fourth, some foreign policy will be a matter of dealing with new situations as they arise, but we should have a picture of the world as we would like to see it in twenty-five years' time, and try to work realistically and patiently towards it.

Of course, we may be diverted, but I think that we have suffered in the last few years by not thinking enough about, for example, the sort of Europe which we should like to see at the end of the century or the kind of relationship which Africans and Europeans should develop. We sometimes seem all too like the population of Syracuse in the days of the tyrant Dion as described by Plutarch when he said: 'They had forgotten they were able to make things happen around them rather than always wait for things to happen to them.'

The fifth point is simply the need for information and its intelligent interpretation. Again referring to the last century, it was doubtless possible for European statesmen to affect a lordly ignorance about the rest of the world. Today, largely due to the revolution in communications and a growing interdependence, nobody can afford to ignore even minor political trends in other parts of the world.

What on first sight may appear to be an innocuous minority movement in any country or continent can suddenly become a focus for international passions, propaganda or exploitation, as for example with Cuba at the time when Castro came to power. Or, Angola after the Portuguese withdrawal. We now know that the Russians and Cubans achieved a decisive victory for the Marxist faction there. Some Western leaders then believed that the Cuban involvement in Africa would stop. But what did we see? We saw the Cuban action repeated in Ethiopia, probably Zaire, and they may have designs on Rhodesia and Namibia.

We must be careful not to choose the interpretation of the facts which arises only from our previous experience. We must approach them with a more open mind, and take into account any new context which may have arisen. As Robert Conquest has said: 'The chief problem today . . . lies in the relationship between our own political culture and ones quite alien to us, with their own history, attitudes, motivations: and the main danger is of applying our own assumptions to quite different mentalities and thus finding ourselves radically misunderstanding the world and conducting policies founded on fantasy.'

My sixth point is that the national character of a people may give a nation historic goals which persist through changing political ideologies. Russian imperialism, for example, was not born in 1917. The history of Russia since the fifteenth century has shown a constant drive to accumulate territory and influence beyond her frontiers. The revolution and civil war barely interrupted this process. Russia was expansionist before, she is expansionist still.

Because any review of foreign policy must of necessity identify the most urgent problems, the picture tends to seem gloomy. Good news is no news. But in fact there are many encouraging signs.

First, the heroic actions of a number of Russian dissidents over the past few years have brought home to us and to some Iron Curtain countries how deep-seated is the desire for liberty and how much can be achieved through resolve, courage and ideals. Solzhenitsyn could not be ignored, nor could his quiet disappearance be arranged. In some ways the pen is still mightier than the sword.

Then we have seen a growing realization by China of the threat that Russia poses to them as well as to us. Indeed, the Chinese criticisms of Russia have been even stronger than some of our Western ones. China is, of course, far from being a member of the golden club of democracies. In philosophical terms, we are as different from her as we are from Russia. But we can recognize that China is not an expansionist power like Russia and she does not pose a threat to us. Our present friendship with China can have only beneficial consequences, both for our people and hers.

Another good sign over the last year or so has been the political evolution in three southern European countries, Spain Portugal and Greece, which, five years ago, still had tough dictatorships. The transition from dictatorship to democracy in Spain and Portugal in particular is one of the few really encouraging things which have occurred.

Again we should not forget that many Third World countries are sympathetic towards the West. In so far as they trade with us and make use of our education, technology and culture, they absorb the customs of political democracy.

Democracy depends on private enterprise as well as on the ballot box, and countries which have the first are more likely to be able to move towards the second. Free enterprise has historically usually preceded freedom, and political freedom has never long survived the end of free enterprise.

Next, among favourable signs, we should not forget that Western technology remains much more inventive than that of the Communist bloc. We may be bad sometimes at following up our own good ideas, bad at keeping secrets, but, looking back over the last generation, it has been Western inventiveness which has shaped the pattern of industrial advance.

Finally in the West we have a closer alliance than has ever been achieved between sovereign states in time of peace. In Nato and the European Community, we have forged new associations between old enemies which have transformed the nature of European politics.

Against the background of these encouraging developments we can identify setbacks and dangers.

First, although we have been the most economically successful countries the world has ever seen, we are not spending enough on defence in relation to the threat we face. Russia has established the largest armoury the world has ever seen, able to challenge the West increasingly by land, sea and air in every part of the world.

Not only does the Soviet Union maintain this vast armament, it maintains it on the basis of an economy incomparably weaker than those of the democracies. Western Europe alone more than matches the GNP of the entire Soviet bloc.

Further, although in the West we have the liberties of which I spoke, we have less of a spirit of resolve, and less of a sense of mission than we used to – less than the Communist countries, which openly boast of their desire to establish their own narrow and tyrannical system throughout the world. Perhaps the poet Yeats put it best when he said: 'The best lack all conviction, while the worst are full of passionate intensity.'

I do not believe that this feeling will endure, but it is a weakness we must face and cure.

When we look at what is happening in the European Community, we find that some of the hopes we have always had for Europe's future are not being fulfilled.

The idea of European unity is a grand concept. But the cause of unity is surely not advanced by hundreds of petty internal regulations, such as on the content of ice-cream or the activities of doorstep salesmen.

Moreover, we need far better machinery for ensuring that Community decisions in matters of trade and finance are in harmony with our European political interests, for example, as they affect Turkey, Yugoslavia, Australia or New Zealand.

To us in Europe these Community decisions may seem detailed economic matters about levies, tariffs and quotas, to be settled as best we can to suit the economic interests of European producers. But these decisions affect, often substantially, the ability of some of our friends overseas to continue as our friends.

We have created an instrument but not yet learned how to use it in our own vital interests.

The Commission and the Council of Ministers need to be more far-sighted, more political in their approach. The Soviet Union would not dream of taking such decisions on technical grounds only.

Perhaps this would be the point to sound a warning about the trend to increased protectionism. This would harm economic growth and political stability in the West and the underdeveloped countries alike.

While we in Europe have our problems, the United States has been through a difficult period in her great history.

The experience of Vietnam, the traumas of Watergate, the open discussion about the activities of the CIA, have meant

that our predominant ally has been through an understand-
able period of doubt and introspection.

But we should be encouraged by what President Carter said
at Annapolis. We should applaud every evidence that the
United States, having taken risks and suffered tragedies which
we did not share, is still determined to play a positive and ima-
ginative part in the world.

I want, in the last part of my talk, to discuss some of the major
problems that we face and how we should approach them.

Defence must be our first consideration. As we have seen in
Britain and elsewhere, there are always politicians ready to
neglect defence in favour of other expenditure which is more
immediately rewarding and which they suppose will therefore
be more popular. I believe that such politicians underestimate
those whom they represent.

Our people are ready to accept the need for stronger
defences because they see these defences not as a provocation
likely to lead to war but as a necessary condition for peace
between East and West. The motorist who fastens his safety
belt cannot be accused of trying to provoke a crash. It is not
firmness but feebleness on the part of the West which could put
a question-mark over the chances of a peaceful world for our
children.

Peace is not best secured by pretending that all is well when
it is not, by saying that Soviet leaders are other than they are,
and that their aims and practices are quite different from what
we know them to be.

The Nato Alliance will always be our best source of security.
Indeed the United States, who will remain the foremost
member of that alliance, has taken the lead in increasing her
own contribution to our joint defences.

But should we not also recall that we have in Brussels the
headquarters of two great organizations, the EEC and Nato,
both concerned with the protection and prosperity of Western
Europe but with little to say to one another. Can that be right?

I understand the difficulties. The membership of the
two organizations is not identical, though overlapping. The

position of France must be respected; the Treaty of Rome does not cover foreign policy or defence.

The friendship of Turkey, for example, is crucial to the West. She has an association agreement with the EEC which needs revising. She might one day become a full member. She is a member of Nato, and it is vital that she remains so. Should not these things be considered together?

The expansion of the Community to include Spain and Portugal might cause certain constitutional problems, but from a defence as well as a political point of view their entry seems a very different matter. It is essential. Yet who is there in the EEC deliberations to speak up for defence?

I feel no assurance that all these connected matters are being looked at together. Where there is so much at stake we cannot tolerate confusion of purpose in the West.

I said earlier that the West should take every opportunity of realistic debate and negotiation with the Soviet Union. I hope that the contacts which exist will in time become more fruitful. As I said publicly in Peking last year, we should continue day-by-day dealings with the Soviet Union and the search for balanced agreements which are of genuine advantage to both sides.

But among ourselves we should be realistic about the conditions of success. The main condition is clear enough. We shall not reach durable understanding with the Soviet Union until she realizes that the West is capable of coherent and resolute protection of its own interests. It is precisely because we wish to avoid confrontation that we need to strengthen our policies.

To that end, we must see our relationship with the Soviet Union as a whole. The supply by the West of credit, grain and technology; the negotiation of different aspects of security and disarmament; Soviet and satellite activities in Africa, Asia and the Pacific, are all features of one landscape.

Unless we learn, as the Soviet Union has learnt, to look at the landscape as a whole we shall be consistently out-manoeuvred.

Our relationship with the Soviet Union cannot be separated from the issue of human rights.

Respect for human rights is the foundation of our democratic way of life. So accustomed are we to this thought that we regard as normal in our countries a degree of respect for human rights which is unparalleled elsewhere in the world. Among the world's sovereign states authoritarian regimes are easier to find than democracies, and among the authoritarian regimes there is an immense variety of attitudes towards the rights of the individual.

For example, a characteristic of Marxist states is the depth and thoroughness of the control exercised over their subjects. They aim to govern thought and faith as well as action. They regard no belief as private, no emotion as beyond their reach, whether about this world or the next, the past or the present.

I have previously mentioned Russian dissidents. The heroic actions of a number of Russian dissidents, like Yuri Orlof, have brought home to us yet again the real nature of the Soviet regime in this post-Stalinist age. Even the Communist parties of Western Europe have criticized it.

There is of course a connection between this thoroughness of control and the long life of these regimes.

We have seen this recently in Europe. Six years ago alongside the Marxist authoritarian regimes in Eastern Europe there were three other dictatorships in Spain, Greece and Portugal. It is no coincidence that all the Marxist regimes remain, while all the others have vanished and have given way to democracy. The former rely not only on military support from the Soviet Union but also on a much more pervasive system of controls.

We must be free from double standards. We must not blind ourselves to contempt for human rights wherever it occurs. The name of Steve Biko is well known as a man who died in the custody of the South African police, and there are numerous accounts of prisoners' sufferings in Chile and Uganda.

But why is the United Nations not examining the atrocities in Cambodia and Ethiopia and the prison camps of Cuba, which no outsiders from the Red Cross or Amnesty International have ever seen?

Any discussion of human rights takes us naturally to consider some of the problems of Africa.

Peace and prosperity throughout the world in the future will be influenced by our ability to solve the problems of Southern Africa. In this, we in the West have a constructive part to play, for we and the countries of the African continent are deeply interdependent.

To ensure her future prosperity Africa needs to develop her raw materials and expand her trade; we need to maintain both our standard of living and our way of life.

I believe that there is not only much good-will towards us but a greater understanding in many countries in Africa of the value to them of trade, technical assistance and investment from the West. In particular, some of them recognize the need to keep in their countries the Europeans whose skills and technology have contributed so much to their economic advance and who are so important to their future.

This is all in marked contrast to the destructive Soviet and Cuban military intervention in Africa and their complete failure to provide any economic assistance.

Let me take Rhodesia as an example of a problem in which we need Western and African understanding. The history of Rhodesia is unique because it has never been under direct rule from Westminster. We have had responsibility with only tenuous power over the years. In spite of this, the world looks to us, even at this late hour, to take the lead in helping black and white Rhodesians to reach peaceful independence based on majority rule. It is an African and Western interest to see a successful settlement. It is a Soviet and Cuban interest to see failure.

But what needs to be recognized by all who seek peace is that the fundamental principle of majority rule was conceded in 1976 after Mr Smith's discussions with Dr Kissinger. The objective of the Executive Council and the four parties to the Salisbury Agreement is to see this principle of majority rule fulfilled. After all, it is black and white Rhodesians who have to live with each other in an independent Rhodesia and it is they who have reached their own internal settlement in Salisbury.

Black Africans in Rhodesia fully acknowledge that the

prosperity of their country depends largely upon the willingness of the whites to stay in that country. It is therefore the views of black and white Rhodesians that really matter.

Here we have the foundations of a lasting settlement. It is a tender plant but one which we must do everything in our power to nourish. Failure to do so will encourage those who believe that they can achieve their objectives only by violence.

Time is running out, but we must do everything in our power to help the Rhodesians to hold free and fair elections by the end of 1978 and to end racial discrimination. And the Patriotic Front must realize that it is in their best interests and those of their country to stop fighting and to participate in these elections.

A peaceful solution in Rhodesia would serve as an encouraging example to South Africa in tackling her own racial problems.

My theme today has been the need for resolution. Resolution to face not shy away from the opportunities, as well as the risks, of a troubled world. Resolution to see international problems as they are and not as we would like them to be, nor as they seemed to be a year, or a decade ago. Resolution to keep our friendships in Europe and across the Atlantic, as Dr Johnson put it, 'in good repair'.

To falter would be to break faith with our heritage.

In the past Europeans have carried free commerce, scientific discovery, the rule of law and democracy itself to the ends of the earth.

But we are more than just an economic or cultural entity, we are a spiritual force or we are nothing. For hundreds of years our story has been bound up with Christianity. It is our taproot to the history of civilization and our link with the future. From it springs our belief in the essential dignity of man and his right to decide his own destiny; our belief in liberty, responsibility, duty and justice.

Together, let us resolve to work for these things, fight for them, live for them.

COMMENTARY

Almost on the threshold of the Conservative victory of 1979, Airey Neave, who had been Margaret Thatcher's adviser during the years of Opposition and particularly at the time of her candidature for the Conservative leadership, was murdered by an Irish terrorist bomb as he was driving out of the House of Commons. The death of this gallant, wise and ingenious man was an immense loss, as Mrs Thatcher acknowledged when giving the first Airey Neave lecture a year later. His death deprived her of advice that would have been invaluable on those occasions, crucial to any government, when it is confronted with wholly unexpected events, and when much hangs on the tactics with which it responds.

In her lecture, Mrs Thatcher paid tribute not only to Airey Neave (whose first Cabinet post would have been Secretary of State for Northern Ireland) but also to the endurance of the Ulster people over years of terrorism. She asserted categorically the government's determination not to capitulate to terrorism, and to maintain the right of the majority in Northern Ireland to remain part of the United Kingdom. But the government has worked persistently for an accommodation in the north with the minority, and for understanding and co-operation with the Republic of Ireland. This has led to resistance by a section of the Unionists, resulting in the tragic situation where policemen have been attacked by Protestant extremists, while the IRA murders have continued. Yet the importance of continuing the efforts to bring the two communities together is absolutely crucial, not least because of the need to reassure opinion in America where the maintenance of investment in Northern Ireland and the extradition of wanted terrorists both probably depend on it.

The main burden of this lecture was once more, however, the role of the state and the right of the individual to freedom from state interference. 'The first principle of this government . . . is to revive a sense of individual responsibility,' the Prime Minister asserted. Yet significantly she also asserted her support for the state as custodian of national traditions, customs and institutions which are not to be justified by abstract logic but because 'over the years they have worked'. She is often misrepresented as a rigid ideologue. In fact, as this speech shows, she understands that a good society is one which is organic and is allowed to grow. The record of her government has shown that although moved by strong convictions, she is not a doctrinaire seeking to govern by blueprints. Any government must move at a pace that carries public opinion with it, which is why Mrs Thatcher's government has been criticized by those who have wanted it to move faster in reforming the post-1945 social service structure, as well as being attacked by those who wish to preserve the status quo.

This lecture carried a clear exposition of the economic illusions which had prevented Britain from facing the world's realities, and which are summed up in the comment that 'basic economic laws can somehow be suspended because we are British'. In the government's early years, the message that disaster lay ahead if these illusions were not discarded met stubborn resistance, not merely from the Opposition parties and the media Establishment of the sixties and seventies, but even from some who were then in the Cabinet itself who feared the political risks. Yet in their hearts the British people had already come to the conclusion that reality must be faced, which is fundamentally why they were to give Mrs Thatcher a second resounding victory in 1983.

The First Airey Neave
Memorial Lecture

LONDON, 3 MARCH 1980

It is now almost a year since Airey Neave was brutally murdered. We have missed him more than we can say. The last ten months have been a time when the party which Airey Neave served so loyally while he lived has been able to begin to put into practice again the ideals for which he stood. Airey would have been as invaluable a counseller in government as he was in opposition. He is irreplaceable.

His long and varied public service began with one of the most famous feats of the Second World War – his escape from Colditz. He learnt much from that extraordinary experience. The prisons of Nazi Germany taught him all that he needed to know about the character of totalitarian rule.

Afterwards, Airey did not have to speculate how a brutal police state behaves when freedom falters: he had himself suffered at the hands of the Gestapo. Nor did he have to read Dostoevsky to know what it means to be told (falsely) that one is about to be court-martialled and shot: it had happened to him.

Airey did not need to study history to know the truth about intolerance, for he had seen Jews being, literally, kicked off the pavement into the street in Munich by SS men. He had seen the Nazi movement at its zenith before the Second World War, with its mass marches and compelling fervour. He also saw that movement in its death throes when, by what he himself described as a strange reversal of fortunes, he, the successful escaped prisoner-of-war, personally served the allied indictment on the major war criminals in their cells at Nuremberg. He later pondered deeply the historical and legal significance of those famous Nuremberg trials at which he played such a remarkable part; and he reached a firm, grave and considered judgement that they did indeed constitute 'a sincere effort to bring compassion and decency to the conduct of war'.

During the war itself, Airey Neave's escape gave him many precious intimations of truth. There is a fine passage in one of his books where he describes how he felt an 'exquisite unburdening of the soul' when he knew that he was, miraculously, outside the prison gates, and free.

Airey went on to tell his readers that escape 'is not a technique but a philosophy.' The real escaper from a prisoner-of-war camp, he said, 'is not just a man equipped with compass, maps and so on.' He 'has an inner self-confidence, a serenity of the spirit which will make him a pilgrim.'

Airey carried that inner confidence and serenity of spirit with him all his life. A philosophy of freedom was an integral part of his character in peace, and in war.

That experienced, thoughtful and valiant fighter for freedom was brutally killed at the end of March 1979, within the precincts of the House of Commons which he loved so well, and where he had so many friends in all parties. That murder, of course, appalled and angered all those friends and the many, many others whom he had throughout the nation. It shocked too all those survivors of Hitler's war to whose cause Airey had devoted so much of his time since 1945.

Airey's death was a severe blow to me. I had come to value his friendship and advice very greatly. That terrible crime may have been intended to disrupt the election. It did not do so. For whatever the sorrow and grief, we were all determined that the election should go ahead normally. The cause which the murderers claimed to support was not advanced in any way by their barbaric violence.

We steadfastly refused to allow this accumulation of menaces to trap us into intolerance. The challenge which the

IRA has been mounting against our political system in Northern Ireland is still being contained by the patience, stoicism and courage of Northern Irish people with the Army and the Royal Ulster Constabulary in the front line. We often use adjectives such as 'heroic' too loosely, but the endurance of Ulster men and women, in the face of danger and over so long, fully entitles them to that designation. We should remember that tonight, as we remember Airey. Nor should we forget that, whenever the terrorists have struck in the homeland of Britain itself, they have met a united response from a nation which has shown once more that, when faced by a clearly identifiable menace, it can respond with wisdom and fortitude.

Despite these years of bloodshed in Ulster, the IRA are no closer to achieving their aims. It is recognized in the Irish Republic and elsewhere that there has always been a clear majority of the population of Northern Ireland which continues to want to remain part of the United Kingdom. A survey carried out in 1978 and published by the Economic and Social Research Institute of Dublin clearly showed that three-quarters of all the people of Northern Ireland, including nearly half the Catholics, wished to retain their links with the United Kingdom. The moral of those findings is worth pondering very seriously. No democratic country can voluntarily abandon its responsibilities in a part of its territory against the will of the majority of the population there. We do not intend to create any precedent of that kind.

I hope that the conference which is now being held in Belfast under the chairmanship of the Secretary of State for Northern Ireland will suggest ways whereby the people of Northern Ireland can, within the United Kingdom, exercise greater responsibility over their own affairs. They want and deserve that opportunity.

We are all conscious of the contribution by Irishmen from North and South to politics and literature over many centuries. Where would even British Conservatism be without the great Edmund Burke, or literature without Sheridan, Shaw, Joyce and Wilde? Englishmen and Irishmen alike have been inspired by Yeats, so that many Irish place names like Innisfree are well known to us even if we have never been to that country.

Nor can we forget the contribution of soldiers from both parts of Ireland in the great wars of this century. In the Second World War 165,000 nationals of the Republic fought for democracy; 750 of them were decorated, of whom eight were awarded the Victoria Cross. The part played by the great generals, Alanbrooke, Alexander, Montgomery, Templer and others, was beyond compare.

Despite our differences over the years, relations between the Republic of Ireland and Britain are still closer than those of most independent sovereign states. Our common membership of the European Community has added an extra dimension to this connection. On the basis of this and our shared past I believe that the United Kingdom and the Republic of Ireland will build a future in friendship.

I spoke a moment ago of the underlying philosophy which Airey Neave believed to be essential in order to make a successful escape from a prison camp.

The political philosophy which guided Airey Neave in his life's work is close to mine. This philosophy does not, and cannot, exactly reflect that of any one great Conservative thinker or statesman of the past, for the obvious reason that our circumstances are utterly different from anything hitherto known.

We read Burke, for example, with pleasure and profit, about the role of the state, but at Burke's death the Civil Service had no more than 16,000 members in all, including sinecures. Even the prisons were privately managed on licence.

The great Lord Salisbury's theory of balance will always assist the thinking of Conservatives. Many of his comments even on the industrial scene may still seem relevant to us: for example, he once spoke in strong sympathy for the movement in favour of an eight-hour working day. He added: 'But from that position to an Act of Parliament telling a man that if he wishes to work ten hours a day he should not do so is a difference as far from the North Pole to the South.'

The great speeches of Winston Churchill will also always inspire Conservatives – as when, after Munich, he adjured the House of Commons 'to say exactly what we think about public affairs . . . this is certainly not the time when it is worth anyone's while to court political popularity.'

It is impossible to know what those or other giants would have said about our problems had they been with us now. Circumstances change but some values are unchanging, and the art of politics is to combine the two. Just as Burke and Salisbury added creatively to tradition for us, so we in our turn must reinterpret and extend those traditions to meet contemporary needs. Future generations will then be able to draw on our experience too.

I have no doubt whatever that the statesmen whose names I have recalled would have been strongly behind the first principle of this government, which is to revive a sense of individual responsibility. It is to reinvigorate not just the economy and industry but the whole body of voluntary associations, loyalties and activities which gives society its richness and diversity, and hence its real strength.

We are convinced that a society of this sort is the best one in which to live.

Since Burke's time the activities of the state have penetrated almost every aspect of life. Among other things the state has become responsible for huge nationalized monopolies employing hundreds of thousands of men and women.

The trouble is that when the state becomes involved in every strike, price or contract affecting a nationalized industry, people tend to associate the state with those things rather than with its higher traditional and necessary role. Consequently its authority is not enhanced, it is diminished.

In our party we do not ask for a feeble state. On the contrary, we need a strong state to preserve both liberty and order, to prevent liberty from crumbling and to keep order from hardening into despotism.

The state has, let us not forget, certain duties which are incontrovertibly its own: for example, to uphold and maintain the law; to defend the nation against attack from without; to safeguard the currency; to guarantee essential services.

We have frequently argued that the state should be more strongly concerned with those matters than it has been. But strong government is quite different from total or absolute government.

A modern Conservative philosopher, Anthony Quinton, put this point in a nutshell: 'What is essential to conservatism is that it should confer absolute power neither on the individual nor the State ... Law is the collective and historical element that is needed to control the actions of individuals, whether rulers or subjects, living and acting in the present.' Further, although ideal government has to be strong, 'it is not charged with the direct control of all the activities of the community.' The Conservative, 'unlike the political theorist of idealism, neither identifies the State with society nor absorbs society within the State.'

The state also is the custodian of national traditions, institutions and customs because they are part of our way of life and our national heritage. They are justified not on any basis of abstract logic – few, if any, of them could have been constructed that way – but because over the years they have worked, and we should be cautious before changing or discarding them.

These are the things which only a government can do and which a government must do. Today, many other services – pre-eminently health and education – are the object of government participation or supervision. But however important, they should not in a free society be government monopolies even though government may be responsible for the larger part.

What we need is a strong state determined to maintain in good repair the frame which surrounds society. But the frame should not be so heavy or so elaborate as to dominate the whole picture. Ordinary men and women who are neither poor nor suffering should not look to the state as a universal provider.

We should remind ourselves of President Kennedy's great injunction: 'Ask not what your country can do for you, but what you can do for your country.' We should not expect the state to appear in the guise of an extravagant good fairy at every christening, a loquacious and tedious companion at every stage of life's journey, the unknown mourner at every funeral.

The relationship between state and people is crucial to our economic approach. Our understanding of economics, our economic philosophy is an extension of our general philosophy.

Airey's philosophy was suffused by a sense of personal responsibility and by a determination not to run away from reality. The two are inseparable. For if, during recent years, we have in Britain done so much less well than we might have done, it is not because we are bad or incompetent, but because a layer of illusion has smothered our moral sense. Let me list a few of the illusions which have blinded us.

The illusion that government can be a universal provider, and yet society still stay free and prosperous.

The illusion that government can print money, and yet the nation still have sound money.

The illusion that every loss can be covered by a subsidy.

The illusion that we can break the link between reward and effort, and still get the reward.

The illusion that basic economic laws can somehow be suspended because we are British.

For years some people have harboured these illusions which have prevented us from facing the realities of the world in which we live. It is time we abandoned them so that we can tackle our problems.

Government and people both have a part to play. For government, facing our national problems entails, above all, keeping the growth in the amount of money in line with the growth in the amount of goods and services. After years of printing too much money, to which the economy has become addicted, this will take time: but it must be done.

But it is not only the total amount of money that matters. It is how that money is distributed between on the one hand the public sector, which produces little real wealth, and on the other hand industry and commerce, the mainstays of our economy.

At present too much is spent on the public sector. It follows that the government's second most important task is to reduce state spending, so that more resources can be put to investment in industry and commerce. This too takes time but it must be done.

Too much money spent by government has gone to support industries which have made and are continuing to make heavy losses. The future requires that industry adapt to produce goods that will sell in tomorrow's world. Older industries that cannot change must be slimmed down and their skills transferred to new products if they are to serve the nation. This too takes time but it must be done.

Economics means harnessing change instead of being dominated by it. But government cannot do it alone. These policies are a necessary but not a sufficient condition for recovery. The British economy is the British people at work – their efforts and their attitudes. Success will only be achieved in so far as people relate the rewards they receive to the efforts they make, and in so far as managers, freed from restrictions imposed by previous governments, respond to their new-found freedom to manage. They and their companies are responsible to those who invest. They are responsible for their fellow employees and responsible to the customer for the quality, delivery and price of their goods. I believe that they are welcoming this new challenge.

Among management and wage-earners alike, there is a widespread sense of relief that the potential of this great people is now matched by the resolve of the government. This was Airey's dream, of a people not dependent on government, but a people exercising initiative independently of government.

This is a daunting but exhilarating mission, one which requires men and women of courage and conviction. We shall see it through. We owe that to our people. We owe it to Airey.

Airey's life encompassed much more than national politics. So I want to say a few words about the international setting of the drama in which we are living in this country. The division of responsibility between state and society of which I have spoken is one of the essential conditions of liberty everywhere. Of course, we need to be sensitive to other cultures, and their traditions. But we believe that they will be best able to reach both happiness and prosperity if they seek similar distinctions.

This belief is the main reason for our scorn for totalitarian societies, whether Nazi, Communist or anything else. For they sought and seek utterly to fuse state and society. They prohibit private associations. They circumscribe religion. They organize culture to conform to the purposes of the state.

We would do well to remember the closing passages of Airey Neave's last book. Recalling that it would be many years before any of us who had lived at that time could begin to forget the Nazis, he reminded us that 'before our eyes the problems of race and terrorism are a frightening reminder of Hitler's example. He lived by terror and his methods appeal to the young and rootless all over the world. Those who use terror to gain their political ends are the heirs of his Revolution of Destruction, however much they may claim to represent opposing doctrines.' How bitter that the man who wrote so clearly about one of the curses of our time should himself die because of it.

Airey Neave looked on the tyrannies which were established in his lifetime in so much of the world, even in Europe, not only as a threat but as a warning. Although deeply English, and devoted to English things, he was not so foolish as to think that tyranny could never be established here. He knew as well as anyone that vigilance is the condition of liberty. He knew too that the Nazis established themselves in a country which had been one of the best educated in the world. He saw only too clearly that despotism persisted after 1945 in another nation – Russia, which for many generations has been territorially the largest state in the world.

That nation now poses the main external threat to our way of life. The Soviet Union is a totalitarian power greater in military strength than was Nazi Germany at the height of the last war. We are seeing in Afghanistan the fulfilment of the warnings which the far-sighted among us have been seeking to give for several years. The threat which the Soviet Union poses indirectly to the West's sources of energy in the Middle East is obvious. Indeed, the continued uncertainty in the Middle East as a whole in the aftermath of the fall of the Shah of Iran offers evident opportunities to the Soviet Union. Whether or not Russia's old desire for a warm-water port in the Indian Ocean was a determining factor in the Soviet decision to invade Afghanistan, that aim is now easier of achievement than it was before. I think that in this country the truth about the growth of Soviet power has been generally appreciated. Increasingly it is now being understood elsewhere and, in this respect, the tragedy of Afghanistan has been salutary. The vote in the General Assembly of the United Nations in January condemning the aggression of the Soviet Union must surely come to be seen as an historic one, perhaps marking the beginning of a more realistic era, in Islam and in the non-aligned world generally.

The increase of realism in domestic affairs seems, therefore, as if it may be balanced by an equal growth of realism internationally. That is encouraging. Sir Isaiah Berlin, in a justly famous study of Russian thinkers during the nineteenth century, wrote that Alexander Herzen considered the destruction of freedom neither inevitable nor, of course, desirable, 'but highly probable unless it was averted by deliberate human effort.' I think we can say that that need for deliberate human effort is more and more realized, at home and abroad.

It would be wishful thinking to make any more claims. We know that we are still in the early stages of our great journey to national recovery. We have a clear notion in our party of our destination. We have a vision of a state which will be more effective because it will be more modest.

We know that once we have conquered our domestic troubles we shall be able to make a more worthy contribution to the safety of the West. We see, in our mind's eye, a nation of responsible citizens proud of their independence, resolved to remain free: worthy of their valiant and true fellow countryman, Airey Neave.

COMMENTARY

*On the morning of Saturday 3 April 1982 the House of
Commons met for an emergency debate on the invasion and
seizure of the Falkland Islands by Argentina. This act of
aggression was in flagrant defiance of the wish of the English-
speaking inhabitants to remain British and of the principle of
self-determination. The Commons was united in condemning
the Argentinian junta, and even the unilateralist left, including
the Labour leader Mr Michael Foot, adopted what a* Times
*leading article described as a 'Churchillian posture'. No doubt
the anger of the Labour Party, which has usually been less
forthright in condemning acts of aggression by leftist governments, was the more intense because the Argentinian junta
could so obviously be described as Fascist. The Opposition
could, and did, also criticize the government for having failed
to react quickly enough to a threat which had been detectable
six weeks earlier, and indeed the Foreign Secretary, Lord
Carrington, and other Foreign Office ministers resigned a few
days later, taking responsibility for the shortcomings with
which their department was charged – namely failure to assess
available intelligence and the junta's intentions more
sensitively.*

*Mrs Thatcher tried to persuade Lord Carrington, in whom
she had great confidence, not to resign. He himself regarded*

most of the criticism as unfounded; nevertheless he insisted on adhering to an honourable tradition of ministerial responsibility which these days is more generally breached than observed. The most substantial charge against the Foreign Office was its failure to send clear signals to Buenos Aires that Britain had the will and the capacity to retake the islands which, had it been understood by the junta, might well have prevented the invasion.

The mood of the whole House of Commons was a virtual endorsement of the decision to send a great mixed task-force to repossess the islands – an enterprise much greater and more hazardous than the original expectation (presumably shared by most MPs that Saturday morning) that a British naval force would simply harass the Argentinian navy in an attempt to force a withdrawal from the Falklands. The success of such a major operation at such a vast distance from Britain was not something that could be taken for granted at the time, and the firmness with which Margaret Thatcher took the decision and then stuck to it did much to solidify the British public's regard for her capacity for decisive leadership and for adherence to principle.

In this case, the principle at stake was a simple but vital one – deterrence, which requires a firm and clear frame of mind even more than adequate weapons. If the Argentine act of aggression were accepted meekly, then although the Falklands did not directly involve Britain's self-interest, there would be a damaging loss of conviction in Britain's will to resist aggression in the broader worldwide struggle for the defence of freedom. In this conflict it was essential that Britain's moral case should have widespread support, and the United Kingdom was sustained by a remarkable degree of support from the European Community, the Commonwealth and especially the United States which, at some sacrifice to its own interest in not alienating South American opinion, gave Britain essential logistical aid. (That help was to be very much in the Prime Minister's mind when she responded to President Reagan's request in 1986 for the use of British bases for the American reprisals on Libya.)

At home, too, there was overwhelming public support. But after its initial explosion of indignation against the Argenti- ~~~~~~*tion. the Labour Party increasingly fell into niggling* ~~~~~~ *complaints that the government was* ~~~~~~ *negotiated settlement. Yet these* ~~~~~~ *ly unconvincing, as the free world's* ~~~~~~ *ed, and they only served to convince* ~~~~~~ *r Party's condemnation of aggression* ~~~~~~ *will to act. Moreover, until the last* ~~~~~~ *nt sought (under United States and* *Uni~~~~* *~~~~~~ es) a peaceful negotiated settlement. Only when it was q~~~~ e clear that this was not available, and that there were too many risks to justify further delay, was the remarkable action launched which liberated the Falklands.*

The 52nd Annual Conservative Women's Conference

LONDON, 26 MAY 1982

Your conference takes place at a time when great and grave issues face our country. Our hearts and minds are focused on the South Atlantic. You have been debating defence policy at a time when our fighting men are engaged in one of the most remarkable military operations in modern times.

We have sent an immensely powerful task-force, more than a hundred ships and 27,000 sailors, marines and soldiers, 8000 miles away in the South Atlantic. In a series of measured and progressive steps, over the past weeks, our forces have tightened their grip on the Falkland Islands. They have retaken South Georgia. Gradually they have denied fresh supplies to the Argentine garrison. Finally, by the successful amphibious landing at San Carlos Bay in the early hours of Friday morning, they have placed themselves in a position to retake the islands and reverse the illegal Argentine invasion.

By the skill of our pilots, our sailors and those manning the Rapier missile batteries on shore they have inflicted heavy losses on the Argentine Air Force – over fifty fixed-wing aircraft have been destroyed.

There have, of course, been tragic losses. You will have heard of the further attacks on our task-force. HMS *Coventry* came under repeated air attack yesterday evening and later sank. One of our Merchant Marine ships, the *Atlantic Con-*

veyor, supporting the task-force, was also damaged and had to be abandoned. We do not yet know the number of casualties but our hearts go out to all those who had men in these ships.

Despite these grievous losses, our resolve is not weakened. We know the reality of war. We know its hazards and its dangers. We know the formidable task that faces our fighting men. They are now established on the Falkland Islands with all the necessary supplies. Although they still face formidable problems in difficult terrain with a hostile climate, their spirits are high.

We must expect fresh attacks upon them, and there can be no question of pressing the Force Commander to move forward prematurely – the judgement about the next tactical moves must be his and his alone.

It was eight weeks ago today that information reached us that the Argentine Fleet was sailing towards the Falklands. Eight thousand miles away . . . At that stage there were only two ways of trying to stop it – through President Reagan, whose appeal to Argentina was rebuffed, and the United Nations, whose plea was also rejected.

There were those who said we should have accepted the Argentine invasion as a *fait accompli*. But whenever the rule of force as distinct from the rule of law is seen to succeed, the world moves a step closer to anarchy.

The older generation in this country, and generations before them, have made sacrifices so that we could be a free society and belong to a community of nations which seeks to resolve disputes by civilized means. Today it falls to us to bear the same responsibility.

What has happened since that day, eight weeks ago, is a matter of history – the history of a nation which rose instinctively to the needs of the occasion.

For decades, the peoples of those islands had enjoyed peace – with freedom, with justice, with democracy. That peace was shattered by a wanton act of armed aggression by Argentina in blatant violation of international law. And everything that has happened since has stemmed from that invasion by the military dictatorship of Argentina.

73

We want that peace restored. But we want it with the same freedom, justice and democracy that the islanders previously enjoyed.

For seven weeks we sought a peaceful solution by diplomatic means: through the good offices of our close friend and ally, the United States; through the unremitting efforts of the Secretary-General of the United Nations.

We studied seven sets of proposals and finally drew up our own. Without compromising fundamental principles, we made a variety of reasonable and practical suggestions in a supreme effort to avoid conflict and loss of life. We worked tirelessly for a peaceful solution. But when there is no response of substance from the other side, there comes a point when it is no longer possible to trust the good faith of those with whom one is negotiating.

Playing for time is not working for a peaceful solution. Wasting time is not willing a peaceful solution. It is simply leaving the aggressor with the fruits of his aggression.

It would be a betrayal of our fighting men and of the islanders if we continued merely to talk, when talk alone was getting nowhere.

And so, seven weeks to the day after the invasion, we moved to recover by force what was taken from us by force. It cannot be said too often: we are the victims; they are the aggressors. As always, we came to military action reluctantly. But when territory which has been British for almost a hundred and fifty years is seized and occupied; when not only British land, but British citizens are in the power of an aggressor, then we have to restore our rights and the rights of the Falkland Islanders.

There have been a handful of questioning voices raised here at home. I would like to answer them. It has been suggested that the size of the Falkland Islands and the comparatively small number of its inhabitants – some 1800 men, women and children – should somehow affect our reaction to what has happened to them.

To those – not many – who speak lightly of a few islanders

The threat of terrorism. *Above:* Mrs Thatcher with her husband Denis at the funeral of Airey Neave. A close adviser and personal friend of the Prime Minister, Airey Neave was murdered by Irish terrorists in the precincts of the Palace of Westminster on 30 March 1979. *Below:* Wearing a red beret of the Parachute Regiment, Mrs Thatcher talks to members of the Welsh Guards at Crossmaglen, Co. Armagh, on Boxing Day 1979.

Above: Celebrating the repossession of the Falkland Islands. Mrs Thatcher is welcomed by men of the Royal Hampshire regiment at Goose Green, January 1983. *Below:* During her six-nation tour of South East Asia Mrs Thatcher met the Indian Prime Minister Rajiv Gandhi in New Delhi, April 1985.

Above: Mrs Thatcher pictured with King Hussein of Jordan during a tour of the Middle East in September 1985 which also included a visit to Egypt. *Below:* Large crowds greeted Mrs Thatcher in Israel on the first official visit ever made by a British Prime Minister in office. *Overleaf:* The leaders of the Western Alliance in Washington, February 1985.

Above: Mrs Thatcher and Mr Teng Hsiao-ping toast the historic Hong Kong agreement in the Great Hall of the People, Beijing (Peking), 19 December 1984. *Below*: Mrs Thatcher was the first Western leader to meet Mikhail Gorbachov, pictured with her here at Chequers in December 1984, four months before Mr Gorbachov became Soviet leader.

Above: Fontainebleau, June 1984. This European Community summit marked the successful outcome of Mrs Thatcher's determined campaign to reach a fair solution to the Community's long-standing budget problem. *Below:* At the following EEC summit meeting held in Dublin in December, Mrs Thatcher is flanked by the Foreign Secretary Sir Geoffrey Howe and the Dutch Foreign Minister Mr Hans van den Broek. *Right:* Vice-President Bush and Mr 'Tip' O'Neill, Speaker of the House of Representatives, applaud Mrs Thatcher after her address to a joint session of the US Congress, 20 February 1985.

Above: The Prime Minister and Foreign Secretary fly out to Beijing in December 1984 to settle the future of Hong Kong. *Below:* The possibility of a Channel tunnel has been discussed for more than a hundred years: on 12 February 1986 Mrs Thatcher and President Mitterrand put their signature to an agreement authorizing the construction of a cross-Channel link.

beyond the seas and who ask the question, 'Are they worth fighting for?' let me say this: right and wrong are not measured by a head-count of those to whom that wrong has been done. That would not be principle but expediency. And the Falklanders, remember, are not strangers. They are our own people. As the Prime Minister of New Zealand, Bob Muldoon, put it in his usual straightforward way, 'With the Falkland Islanders, it is family.'

When their land was invaded and their homes were overrun, they naturally turned to us for help, and we, their fellow citizens, 8000 miles away in our much larger island, could not and did not beg to be excused. We sent our men and our ships with all speed, hoping against hope that we would not have to use them in battle but prepared to do so if all attempts at a peaceful solution failed. When those attempts failed, we could not sail by on the other side.

And let me add this. If we, the British, were to shrug our shoulders at what has happened in the South Atlantic and acquiesce in the illegal seizure of those far-away islands, it would be a clear signal to those with similar designs on the territory of others to follow in the footsteps of aggression.

Surely we, of all people, have learnt the lesson of history: that to appease an aggression is to invite aggression elsewhere, and on an ever-increasing scale.

Other voices — only a few — have accused us of clinging to colonialism or even imperialism. Let me remind those who advance that argument that the British have a record second to none of leading colony after colony to freedom and independence. We cling not to colonialism but self-determination.

Still others — again only a few — say we must not put at risk our investments and interests in Latin America; that trade and commerce are too important to us to put in jeopardy some of the valuable markets of the world.

But what would the Falklanders, under the heel of the invader, say to that? What kind of people would we be if, enjoying the birthright of freedom ourselves, we abandoned British citizens for the sake of commercial gain?

Now we are present in strength on the Falkland Islands.

Our purpose is to repossess them. We shall carry on until that purpose is accomplished.

When the invader has left, there will be much to do – rebuilding, restoring homes and farms, and above all renewing the confidence of the people in their future. Their wishes will need time to crystallize, and of course will depend in some measure on what we and others are prepared to do to develop the untapped resources and safeguard the Islands' future.

Madam Chairman, our cause is just. It is the cause of freedom and the rule of law. It is the cause of support for the weak against aggression by the strong.

Let us then draw together in the name, not of jingoism but of justice. And let our nation, as it has so often in the past, remind itself, and the world:

Nought shall make us rue,
If England to herself do rest but true.

COMMENTARY

Shortly after the successful end of the Falklands conflict Margaret Thatcher gave her first address to the General Assembly of the United Nations. Very appropriately it was at a Special Session on disarmament. The theme of the speech was deterrence, and although there was no direct reference to the Falklands war, there were between the lines many implied allusions to the lessons that could be drawn from it. The Prime Minister came to the United Nations with the self-assurance of a victor and was heard as such. But she also came as a representative of a country which had learnt the hard way the consequences of not making its determination to resist force clear enough to deter aggression.

The Falklands affair could almost have been designed by fate as a vivid and tragic small-scale illustration of the defence philosophy outlined in this speech, the theme of which was clear and coherent. The purpose of defence is to preserve peace with freedom, and nuclear weapons, because they allow no victors, have prevented a world war by deterrence – even though, as Mrs Thatcher pointed out, ten million people had been killed in so-called conventional conflicts since Nagasaki. Disarmament and arms controls must be pursued vigorously, she maintained, and what could be achieved was illustrated by such agreements as the Non-Proliferation Treaty and the ban on biological (though not yet, alas, chemical) weapons. But the essence of disarmament was verification, and peace could only be assured by recognizing that wars were caused, not by the existence of particular weapons or by the arms race, but by the belief of aggressors that they could change things by using force, and get away with an easy victory.

The cost in human lives of proving the aggressor wrong after the aggression was much greater than preventing his action in the first place. Here the Prime Minister referred to Hitler, but she could equally have referred to General Galtieri who admitted in so many words after it was all over that he would never have acted as he did had it been seriously thought that Britain would respond as she did. Indeed, those who criticized the Foreign Office at the time took the view that it had regarded the Falkland Islands as an inconvenience and a distraction which could not in the long run be defended. The critics also felt that because the Foreign Office had been preoccupied with negotiating an agreement with the Argentines for disposing of the problem on terms acceptable to Parliament, the junta had been given the idea that if we were confronted with a fait accompli *we might accept it with a few protests and gestures, before agreeing to something acceptable to Buenos Aires.*

In others words, there was a failure to apply the principle of deterrence which is applicable as much to conventional as to nuclear defence. It is also worth remembering that the Labour Party, after its initial protest against the invasion and support for action, gradually disengaged from government policy, largely because of pressure from its left-wingers who had not even wanted the expedition to start. Michael Foot therefore constantly recommended a return to the UN before any action, declaring that we must not 'torpedo' peace. 'If one initiative fails, another must be started,' he insisted, which raised the question of how many 'initiatives' he thought should be taken and with how much delay. It began to look as though the Labour Party would have continued the initiatives indefinitely while the task-force was rendered incapable of action by delay and a vicious winter. Now, however, the expedition had been brought to a successful conclusion, and after her address to the United Nations and a visit to President Reagan the Prime Minister could tell a press conference in Washington that the only people with whom Britain would discuss sovereignty were the islanders themselves.

In one further respect these events marked a watershed for Margaret Thatcher. Hitherto she had been largely preoccupied with the desperate fight at home against inflation, leaving diplomacy in the experienced hands of Lord Carrington. With his departure, she herself moved much more to the forefront of international affairs, and her speech to the United Nations represents the fullest account of her approach to policy she had yet given.

The United Nations General Assembly

NEW YORK, 23 JUNE 1982

The stated purpose of this Special Session is disarmament. The underlying and more important purpose is peace – not peace at any price, but peace with freedom and justice. As President Roosevelt commented during the last war: 'We, born to freedom and believing in freedom, would rather die on our feet than live on our knees.'

Leaders of countries from every part of the globe come to this Session in search of surer ways of preserving that peace – ways that enable the peoples of each sovereign state to lead their lives as they choose within established borders. If arms control helps us to achieve those central aims more surely and at less cost we must pursue it vigorously. But if it is carried out in a way which damages peace we must resist it, recalling that there have been occasions when the known or perceived military weakness of an opponent has been at least as potent a cause of war as military strength. The true definition of disarmament should be 'the balanced and verifiable reduction of armaments in a manner which enhances peace and security'.

Discussion of disarmament inevitably turns to the weapons of war. Our generation faces a special responsibility, because the march of modern technology has made ever more deadly the weapons of war. We are most keenly aware of that in the case of nuclear weapons because of their terrifying destructive power which my generation has witnessed and which none of us will ever forget. However alarmed we are by those weapons, we cannot disinvent them. The world cannot cancel the knowledge of how to make them. It is an irreversible fact. Nuclear weapons must be seen as deterrents. They contribute to what Winston Churchill called 'a balance of terror'. There would be no victor in a nuclear exchange. Indeed, to start a war among nuclear powers is not a rational option. These weapons succeed in so far as they prevent war. And for thirty-seven years nuclear weapons *have* kept the peace between East and West. That is a priceless achievement.

Provided there is the will and good sense, deterrence can be maintained at substantially reduced levels of nuclear weapons. Of course we must look for a better system of preventing war than nuclear deterrence. But to suggest that between East and West there is such a system within reach at the present time would be a perilous pretence.

For us the task is to harness the existence of nuclear weapons to the service of peace, as we have done for half a lifetime. In that task the duty of the nuclear powers is to show restraint and responsibility. The distinctive role of the non-nuclear countries, I suggest, is to recognize that proliferation of nuclear weapons cannot be the way to a safer world.

Nuclear weapons were a major concern of the 1978 Special Session; and they must remain so for us. But they may mask the facts about what we sometimes call, too comfortably, conventional weapons and conventional war. Since Nagasaki there have been no conflicts in which nuclear weapons have been used. But there have been something like 140 conflicts fought with conventional weapons, in which up to ten million people have died.

Nuclear war is indeed a terrible threat; but conventional war is a terrible reality. If we deplore the amount of military spending in a world where so many go hungry and so much else needs to be done, our criticism and our action should turn above all to conventional forces which absorb up to 90 per cent of military spending worldwide.

We are all involved – we all have conventional forces. I am

convinced that we need a deeper and wider effort throughout the non-nuclear field, to see what we can do together to lighten the risks, the burdens and the fears.

But in a crucial sense, Mr President, we have not reached the root of the matter. For the fundamental risk to peace is not the existence of weapons of particular types, it is the disposition on the part of some states to impose change on others by resorting to force. This is where we require action and protection. And our key need is not for promises against first use of this or that kind of military weapon – such promises can never be dependable amid the stresses of war. We need a credible assurance, if such can ever be obtained, against starting military action at all. The leaders of the North Atlantic Alliance have just given a solemn collective undertaking to precisely that effect. They said: 'None of our weapons will ever be used except in response to attack.'

Let us face the reality. The springs of war lie in the readiness to resort to force against other nations, and not in 'arms races', whether real or imaginary. Aggressors do not start wars because an adversary has built up his own strength. They start wars because they believe they can gain more by going to war than by remaining at peace. Few, if any, of the 140 conflicts since 1945 can be traced to an arms race. Nor was the world war of 1939–45 caused by any kind of arms race. On the contrary, it sprang from the belief of a tyrant that his neighbours lacked the means or the will to resist him effectively. Let us remember what Bismarck said, some seventy years earlier: 'Do I want war? Of course not – I want victory.' Hitler believed he could have victory without war, or with not very much or very difficult war. The cost to humanity of disproving that belief was immense; the cost of preventing him from forming it in the first place would have been infinitely less.

The causes which have produced war in the past have not disappeared today, as we know to our cost. The lesson is that disarmament and good intentions on their own do not ensure peace.

Mr President, there is a national revulsion in democratic societies against war and we would much prefer to see arms build-ups prevented, by good sense or persuasion or agreement. But if that does not work, then the owners of these vast armouries must not be allowed to imagine that they could use them with impunity.

Mere words, speeches and resolutions will not prevent them. The security of our country and its friends can be ensured only be deterrence and by adequate strength – adequate when compared with that of a potential aggressor.

I have explained why in general I do not believe that armaments cause wars and why action on them alone will not prevent wars. It is not merely a mistaken analysis but an evasion of responsibility to suppose that we can prevent the horrors of war by focusing on its instruments. These are more often symptoms than causes.

I have made these points not in any way to decry disarmament and arms control – I believe in them both – but to make quite clear what they can and cannot achieve. Excessive claims and demands have too often been not an aid to practical measures, but a substitute for them. Arms control alone cannot remove the possibility of war. Nevertheless the limitation and reduction of armaments can still do a great deal. They can reduce the economic burden of military preparation for legitimate self-defence. They can diminish the inhumanity of conflict. They can restrict the military use of advancing science and technology. They can ease tension between states and lessen the fears of people everywhere. To do these things, and to do them in a way that is balanced, verifiable and dependable, is worth sustained and persistent endeavour.

Critics too often play down what has already been done through arms control agreements, whether formal or informal – such agreements as those on outer space, the sea bed, Antarctica, the Partial Test Ban Treaty, the Non-Proliferation Treaty, and the various Geneva Accords over the years.

My country was among the architects of some of these successes. Although a Comprehensive Test Ban Treaty has not been signed and the recent review of the Non-Proliferation Treaty was unproductive, there has been no additional nuclear weapon state since 1964. We also contributed substantially to the banning of biological and toxin weapons in 1972.

We all wish that the achievements had been greater. But to suggest that what has been done so far is insignificant, is both inaccurate and unhelpful to further progress. We have a useful foundation upon which to build. Now we must go a stage further.

In the nuclear field, the hopes of the world lie in direct talks between the United States and the Soviet Union, the countries which have by far the largest arsenals. These could be greatly reduced in a way which would not endanger security. Decisive action is needed, not just declarations or freezes. I welcome the radical proposals made by the United States for substantially cutting strategic weapons, and for eliminating a whole class of intermediate-range systems (the zero option). The negotiations deserve the whole-hearted support of us all.

We are also deeply concerned about the dangers of chemical warfare. When the world community decided in 1972 to ban the possession of biological and toxin weapons, we all looked forward to corresponding action next on chemical weapons. It has not happened. Moreover, there is reason to doubt whether every country which signed the 1972 Treaty is observing it. There have been disquieting and well-documented reports, which urgently need investigation, that chemical weapons and toxins have been used in some countries in Asia. The Committee on Disarmament needs to give renewed and determined impetus to a properly verifiable convention banning development and possession of such weapons.

I spoke earlier about the huge weight of conventional forces. The biggest concentration and confrontation of such forces anywhere in the world lies in Europe. But it is heavily weighted on the side of the Warsaw Pact. This situation is in itself a cause for concern.

But there is the more fundamental question whether the Warsaw Pact can or wishes to sustain a stable relationship with the rest of the world. Do not the events in Poland and Afghanistan call this into question, the one by revealing deep disillusion within the Soviet Empire, the second by demonstrating the Soviet propensity to extend its frontiers? Both are evidence of an underlying instability. Thus the need to secure a better balance in conventional arms becomes even more imperative.

For nine years we have pursued patiently talks in Vienna on mutual and balanced force reductions. Our diplomats involved in those talks must be the most patient of all, but they know that their work is of vital importance for peace. Fresh proposals are being made and we hope that this time we shall see some progress.

Britain would also like to see a special effort made to agree on new mandatory confidence and security-building measures in Europe. These would be a valuable complement to action in Vienna on force levels.

Through all these many negotiations there runs a critical factor – verification. How can we be sure that what it is said will be done, is done? Where national security is at stake we cannot take agreements on trust, especially when some states are so secretive and such closed societies. Agreements which cannot be verified can be worse than useless – they can be a new source of danger, fear and mistrust. Verification is not an optional extra in disarmament and arms control. It is the heart of the matter.

Differences over verification have often proved a stumbling block in arms control negotiations. But we note that the Soviet Union is now prepared to open part of its civil nuclear installations to inspection by the International Atomic Energy Agency – a step that the United Kingdom took years ago. I note also that the Soviet Union now seems ready to accept the need for systematic on-site inspection in respect of a chemical weapons treaty. We need to redouble our efforts to bridge the gaps that still remain.

Britain's record over the years in work on disarmament and arms control stands up to any comparison. We wish to do more – not by rhetoric, still less by propaganda postures, but by steady, relevant work going step by step through these difficult and complex matters. This is a long, patient and unspectacular business. There is no short cut if we are to retain security and peace.

These are the considerations which I suggest the Special Session needs to have in mind in discussing a Comprehensive Programme of Disarmament and in its review of progress since the first Special Session.

The message I bring is practical and realistic. It is the message of a country determined to preserve and spread the values by which we live. It contains nought of comfort to those who seek only a quiet life for themselves at the expense of the freedom of others, nor to those who wish to impose their will by force. Peace and security require unbroken effort.

We believe that the human values of civilization must be defended.

We believe that international law and the United Nations Charter must be upheld.

We believe that wars are caused not by armaments but by the ambitions of aggressors and that what tempts them is the prospect of easy advantage and quick victory.

We believe that the best safeguard of peace lies not only in a just cause but in secure defence.

We believe in balanced and verifiable disarmament where it can be the servant of peace and freedom.

We believe that the purpose of nuclear weapons should be to prevent war and that it can be achieved by smaller armouries.

We believe that a balanced reduction in conventional weapons could create greater stability.

We believe we have a right and a duty to defend our own people whenever and wherever their liberty is challenged.

Mr President, my country seeks the path of peace with freedom and justice. As Abraham Lincoln put it in his second Inaugural Address, 'With malice towards none, with charity for all, with firmness in the right . . . Let us strive on to finish the work we are in . . .'

COMMENTARY

In September 1983 Margaret Thatcher spoke in Washington at a British Embassy dinner during which she was presented with the Winston Churchill Foundation award, and it was in tones almost reminiscent of those in which Churchill himself had given warning of the perils threatening from the enemies of his time that she spoke of the dangers from the Soviet Union. Accusing Moscow of presiding over 'a modern version of the early tyrannies of history', the Prime Minister gave warning that the West was 'confronted by a power of great military strength, which has consistently used force against its neighbours, which wields the threat of force as a weapon of policy, and which is bent on subverting and destroying the confidence and stability of the Western world.'

Since the Falklands war the personal understanding between President Reagan and Mrs Thatcher had grown much closer. This was despite the fact that the Prime Minister and the British Cabinet did not conceal their disapproval of the maintenance of high US budget deficits which led to high interest rates, and therefore to the continuance of higher than necessary interest rates in Britain and elsewhere at the expense of growth. As Mrs Thatcher said in her speech, the differences between Britain and the US were nothing compared to what the two countries shared.

Her understanding with the President had been particularly significant at a time when a strong political campaign was being waged in Europe against the siting of cruise missiles. What is more, it had obviously become harder for the democratic West, facing recession, rising costs and smaller resources, to insist on finding the money for defence at the expense of social spending, than it was for the Soviet Union with no electorate to face. The need to remind people of the nature of the threat is one that the West cannot afford to forget, and Mrs Thatcher has done her share in reminding us of this reality.

On the day of the British Embassy dinner, Mrs Thatcher had had a long meeting with President Reagan as well as talks with senior members of the American administration. Afterwards she reiterated Britain's determination to go ahead with the deployment of cruise missiles at the end of that year. She also emphasized that she wanted the negotiations on reducing intermediate nuclear missiles in Europe to continue towards a planned and verifiable agreement. She rejected suggestions that the British and French deterrents should be included in the IMF talks on the grounds that Britain had Polaris long before any IMF missiles were stationed in Europe.

At the heart of her British Embassy address was again the need to be willing, and to be seen to be willing, to defend freedom, as well as to recognize the Soviet Union's obedience to a wholly different ethic and its willingness to use force to dominate its neighbours in the alleged interest of progress. (Mrs Thatcher cited as an instance of Soviet ruthlessness the shooting down of the Korean airliner less than a month previously.) Not the least interesting part of her speech was her declaration of willingness to engage in the battle of ideas for the hearts of mankind, which had recently been stated as an objective by the then Russian leader, Mr Andropov. It is at this point that one can see clearly the link between her foreign policy and the theme of her domestic policy, which has been to invite the British people to consider the proposition that Socialism in any true sense, even when watered down to fit in to a democratic and parliamentary framework, is in the long run inevitably in some state of tension with freedom.

The Winston Churchill Foundation Award Dinner

WASHINGTON, 29 SEPTEMBER 1983

I am deeply grateful to the Winston Churchill Foundation of the United States for honouring me with this award.

It is my great pride that when I first entered the House of Commons nearly twenty-five years ago Winston Churchill was still a member. I remember him then, small, a little deaf, a little hunched, yet towering above the rest of us as he has done ever since. He was always concerned to keep the courtesies of the House. I remember the day when he left it. Supported by two friends he slowly turned and for the last time bowed to the Speaker and to the Parliament he loved. Then he was gone.

No one, least of all a Conservative Prime Minister, can receive an award that bears his name without an abiding sense of humility. In doing so, I am conscious that Churchill belongs to you in the United States as well as to us in the United Kingdom.

He began life with an American mother and an English father. By the end of his life he had been made Honorary American Citizen by the United States Congress. At his funeral the great 'Battle Hymn of the Republic' was sung. Churchill knew before his death that you had set up this splendid foundation as a tribute to him.

Already eight of your Churchill Fellows have won Nobel prizes. I congratulate you on that magnificent achievement.

The presence of the Churchill Fellows in Cambridge helps to sustain and enrich the close personal links between the United Kingdom and the United States which are the bedrock of our enduring friendship. Nothing would have delighted Churchill more.

He was a giant. He saw clearly, he warned clearly, he did what had to be done. His steadfast attachment to fundamental principles, his heroic indifference to the pressures and expediencies of the moment, and his unbending determination both saved his own country and helped to save the world. It was he who said: 'Once you take the position of not being able in any circumstances to defend your rights against . . . aggression . . . there is no end to the demands that will be made or to the humiliations that must be accepted.'

True in the face of the Nazi menace in the 1930s. True in the face of the threats to our way of life today. True, too, in the South Atlantic last year when with the most heartwarming support and encouragement of the people of America, Britain again had to demonstrate that aggression must not be allowed to succeed and that international law and the right of people freely to choose their own way of life must be upheld.

The best memorial we can offer to the life of that man of destiny is to treasure the matchless gift of freedom which his leadership preserved for us and to pass it on to generations yet to come, both in those countries which already know freedom and those which yearn for it.

That is the great role of the Western democracies in this age. It is our duty to understand the threat we face, to be strong enough to deter any aggressor, to engage in and win the battle of ideas and, as Churchill always sought to do, to bind ever more closely those nations which cherish the dignity of man and the power of the human spirit.

First, the threat. We have to deal with the Soviet Union. But we must deal with it not as we would like it to be, but as it is. We live on the same planet and we have to go on sharing it. We stand ready therefore – if and when the circumstances are right – to talk to the Soviet leadership.

But we must not fall into the trap of projecting our own morality on to the Soviet leaders. They do not share our aspirations: they are not constrained by our ethics, they have always considered themselves exempt from the rules that bind other states. They claim to speak in the name of humanity, but they oppress the individual. They pose as the champion of free nations, but in their own empire they practise total control. They invoke the word democracy, but they practise single-party rule by a self-appointed oligarchy. They pretend to support the freedom of the ballot-box, but they are protected by a system of one man, one vote – and one candidate.

Their power is sustained by myth. Presenting themselves to the world as the fount of progress and revolution, they preside over a modern version of the early tyrannies of history – a structure so rigid that it totally precludes the normal processes of questioning, discussion and change.

They have little contact with their own people, still less with the free world.

This would-be revolutionary power has an unparalleled arsenal of nuclear and conventional weapons at its disposal. Its governing principles are force and dictatorship. It sees the expansion of Communism as inevitable, a logical step in the march of history, and the rest of the world as its rightful fiefdom.

We have watched the depredations of the Soviet Union in the sixty-six years since its creation. While the Soviet Union has imposed its rule on its neighbours and drawn an Iron Curtain between East and West, we in Great Britain have given freedom and independence to more than forty countries whose populations now number more than one thousand million – a quarter of the world's total.

The readiness of Russia to use force outside its borders is manifest. It is active in every continent, reaching deep into the domestic affairs of independent countries – openly or covertly, by using the tools of subversion.

Less than a month ago, we saw fresh evidence of the nature of the system with which we have to deal. The destruction of the Korean airliner was an act of atrocity, and of profound contempt for their fellow human beings.

Mr Chairman, it is disturbing but not surprising that the system I have described should be capable of such acts. The lesson for us is that our policies should recognize that system for what it is.

We are confronted by a power of great military strength, which has consistently used force against its neighbours, which wields the threat of force as a weapon of policy, and which is bent on subverting and destroying the confidence and stability of the Western world. That is the threat we face. What is our response?

After the Second World War, when optimism gave way to the sombre realization that the democracies faced a new danger, a few far-sighted men, inspired by the war-time collaboration of Churchill and Roosevelt, established the Western Alliance.

Its aim was then, and remains today, entirely defensive – to safeguard the democratic ideals and way of life of its members.

Its membership was then, and remains today, entirely voluntary. It has been an unqualified success. The member countries of Nato have preserved their freedom and provided material prosperity for their people on a scale that only fifty years ago would have seemed like a dream. And peace has reigned secure.

Why? Because potential aggressors know that we in the West are strong and that we have the will to use that strength to defend what we believe. Does it need saying that the Soviet Union has nothing to fear from us? For several years after the war the United States had a monopoly of nuclear weapons, but was a threat to no one. Democracies are naturally peace-loving. There is so much which our people wish to do with their lives, so many uses for our resources other than military equipment. The use of force and the threat of force to advance our beliefs are no part of our philosophy. The radical proposals for disarmament come from the West. It is the response from Moscow which is deficient. This week we have seen yet again genuine proposals from the West peremptorily rejected.

No amount of propaganda, of spurious half-truths, can disguise the determination of the Soviet Union to maintain or gain numerical advantage in weaponry, men and materials.

No amount of facile argument can conceal the fact that Soviet flexibility to date has been designed to beguile public opinion, not to make progress by genuine negotiation at Geneva.

Some may recoil at the thought of negotiating with men whose theories and actions have been responsible for so much suffering. Yet the character of modern weapons, not only nuclear but conventional, obliges us to do so. So we must persist in our efforts, but resolved to do nothing that would hand an advantage to the other side, nothing to put at risk the credibility of the Western Alliance, and nothing to unsettle that military balance on which peace itself depends.

Mr Chairman, the facts of nuclear life have, we profoundly hope, ruled out war as an instrument of national policy – provided of course that there is no military weakness on our side which would tempt the other into ill-considered action.

But there is another battle. In June 1983 Mr Andropov told the Central Committee of the Communist Party: 'A struggle is under way for the minds and hearts of billions of people on the planet, and the future of mankind depends, to a considerable extent, on the outcome of this ideological struggle.'

That is Mr Andropov's challenge. I accept it, and I do so with the confidence which Winston Churchill would have shared, that in this battle we in the West hold the cards.

Here, in the West, the peoples of the world find creative thinking, creative art and inventive genius, standards of excellence in literature and music, indeed in that whole great area of human reflection and expression that we call culture.

It is to the West that friend and foe come for investment capital, grain supplies, science and technology, medical research, methods to protect the environment and to preserve wildlife – and for so much else. People turn to the West because we are free. It is our human values to which men aspire.

'You in the West,' said a Hungarian poet, 'have a special duty because you are free. That freedom is both a blessing and a burden, for it makes you spiritually responsible for the whole of humanity.' He was right. For if we do not keep alive the flame of freedom, that flame will go out, and every noble ideal will die with it. It is not by force of weapons, but by force of ideas that we seek to spread liberty to the world's oppressed. It is not only ideals, but conscience that impels us to do so.

Is there conscience in the Kremlin? Do they ever ask themselves what is the purpose of life? What is it all for? Does the way they handled the Korean airliner atrocity suggest that they ever considered such questions?

No. Their creed is barren of conscience, immune to the promptings of good and evil. To them it is the system that counts, and all men must conform.

Nevertheless in Poland they have seen that Communism, even when disguised as military government, cannot suppress the soul of the people. Do they ever wonder, nay even fear, whether the day will not dawn when their own people will give voice to their feelings and frustrations?

Freedom of conscience is a natural right which laws did not give and which law can never take away.

It is the countries of the democratic West which recognize the limits of the power of the state, and which enshrine the conscience of man in the very structure of their institutions. It is this which is the burden of our responsibility to mankind. Surely this was what Churchill meant when he said in a wartime broadcast to this country: 'United we can save and guide the world. Divided the dark ages return.'

Those words are as true today as they were in June 1941.

Our ideals and our values are our living strength. Soviet ideology teaches that we in the West are like ripe apples, ready to fall into their laps: that all they have to do is shake the tree.

As someone else might have said: 'Some apple, some tree.'

Mr Chairman, I yield to Winston Churchill in many things but not in his admiration and affection for this country. The American commitment to freedom is the linchpin of the West. You have shown incomparable generosity to others, as we in Europe have good cause to know. By promoting post-war economic recovery through the Marshall Plan, by offering the shattered European democracies your military protection, by contributing your resolve and strength to the Western Alliance, you have made possible that remarkable renaissance of Western Europe which stands in such stark contrast to the Eastern half of our continent.

Differences between us? Yes, we have a few, but they are as nothing compared with the things we share – our resolve to defend our way of life, to deter all threats and to ensure in the end that triumph of freedom which America and Britain work for, long for and believe will one day come.

Mr Chairman, I began with Winston Churchill, and I will end with him. Who better? Churchill wrote: 'Where we are able to stand together and work together for righteous causes, we shall always be thankful, and the world will always be free.'

COMMENTARY

If one pillar of Margaret Thatcher's foreign policy is the alliance with the United States within Nato, the other has been the political importance of the Community of free European nations which works for the same purpose – upholding freedom. Yet there were times when she did not seem an enthusiastic 'European'. She had fought a long and often acrimonious battle to obtain permanent arrangements by which the United Kingdom should be compensated for its excessively large contributions to the European budget. She was often criticized by over-respectful British adherents of the Brussels establishment of 'banging the table'. Softer diplomatic talk, they said, would have served better. They were wrong. By the summer of 1984, an agreement of principle was in sight, with only comparatively small differences over figures to be settled.

Settlement was reached at the European summit at Fontainebleau in June, and in exchange Britain agreed to raise the ceiling of the VAT-related contributions to the European Community's 'own resources' without which there would have been financial crisis which could conceivably have broken the Community. But also on the table at Fontainebleau was a so-called draft Treaty of Union, proposing a great deal of supranational constitution-building (including the loss of the national 'veto' in cases of a member state's vital interest) which was simply not feasible in the real world of nation-states, which the Community comprises. Other nations paid lip-service to this notion; the British did not, preferring an approach which was both more pragmatic and effective, and which was based on the political as well as the economic realities.

At Fontainebleau, Mrs Thatcher had presented her fellow heads of state with a paper outlining her own views and stressing the future need to present the Community in a 'more favourable light'. Specifically, this allegedly 'bad' European insisted that the EEC must progressively 'aim beyond the Common Commercial Policy through political co-operation towards a common approach to external affairs.' It should 'adopt common positions on world problems and . . . vote together in non-economic international bodies.' It should speak collectively to the US on commercial questions, and have a coherent voice on East–West relations.

Such was the background against which Mrs Thatcher delivered a speech to the Franco-British Council dinner at Avignon a few days before another summit meeting of the European Council, which was this time to be preoccupied with the complexities of wine and fish in the light of the admission of Spain and Portugal. Again she made her views crystal clear. What she dislikes about the Community (as do so many ordinary British people) are its complex bureaucratic regulations. Her aim is a genuinely free internal market. She wants it to be an outward-looking body, as strong and self-confident as the United States, and with correspondingly self-confident currencies. Once again she made it clear that she did not think that Europe could ever have 'union' as the Americans know it; our history is too different. But we can have unity. That theme (a development of what she said at Brussels in 1978) contains much more realism than the drawing up of blueprints for the kind of union about which so many Europeans like to fantasize.

The Franco–British Council Dinner

AVIGNON, 30 NOVEMBER 1984

European. Nations. Both words are important.

'Nations': both France and Britain share a fierce and distinctive sense of national identity. We have both traditionally placed a high value on national independence. And what is wrong in that? As G. K. Chesterton said:

All good men are international
And if we are to be international,
We must be national.

But the word 'European' is important too. Our cultures and national traditions both spring from Europe.

How to deal with Europe, what to make of Europe, has been a dominant theme in both our histories. Sometimes the answer was a bid for domination – or a bid to prevent it. At other times, we spent our energy on pursuing interests and ambitions outside Europe. Sometimes the story was one of co-operation, sometimes competition, sometimes even collision.

Today, Britain and France are steering very much in the same direction. We should be looking for ways to work together more closely still. Just a few days before a European Council the first and most obvious place to look is the European Community.

Of one thing I am certain: the Community's founding fathers would be horrified at the labyrinth of its bureaucratic regulations which entwine us like Gulliver pinned down by the little men of Lilliput. Horrified because the Treaty of Rome embodies the economic structure of a free society.

The very first paragraphs of that Treaty speak of 'the progressive abolition of restrictions on international trade . . . elimination of the barriers which divide Europe . . . abolition of obstacles to freedom of movement for persons, services and capital . . . a system ensuring that competition in the Common Market is not distorted . . . the association of the overseas countries and territories in order to increase trade.' The Community was formed to expand trade, not to protect home markets. It was conceived as an outward looking body, not one obsessed with the minutiae of its internal procedures. Britain and France, as countries which have both known empires and brought them to independence, have a special duty to preserve that characteristic.

What a long way short of those original goals we still are. To take but one or two examples. Why cannot we make it as cheap for our citizens to travel by air within their own continent as they can to other continents? Why cannot it be as easy for German businessmen to take out insurance direct at Lloyds of London as it is for British motorists to buy German cars?

Many years ago that great character Ernest Bevin was asked what the aim of his foreign policy really was. His reply: 'To go down to Victoria Station, get a railway ticket and go where the hell I like without a passport or anything else.' That emphasis on breaking down barriers, on taking measures which benefit directly our ordinary citizens, must be our priority in Europe. We look forward to receiving practical proposals from the Committee on a People's Europe set up at the European Council in Fontainebleau.

In the Community at present, much attention is focused on the strength of the US dollar – and not surprisingly because it affects us all. Clearly a deficit approaching $200 billion and the high real interest rates needed to attract savings from the rest of the world are a major factor. But the dollar stays strong despite a burgeoning federal debt and a widening current account deficit because people the world over have confidence in the permanence and stability of the free enterprise society of the United States. They know that economic freedom is the foundation for political freedom and that neither are in danger. So it is in the dollar that they invest for the long term – a bottom drawer investment.

There is a lesson there for Europe. Is it not possible that the long-term strength of the dollar is due in part to uncertainties about the future direction of Europe? That our currencies will only rival the dollar as a safe haven when investors conclude that economic freedom and an enterprise culture are as strongly entrenched in Europe as they are in the United States? I might also add that Europe needs to rival the United States in the speed with which it both creates and accepts technological change.

Mr Chairman, Europe will only be strong and able to play its rightful part in the world when it attains the economic freedom which was the vision of the authors of the Treaty of Rome.

Several distinguished Europeans gave me advice on what to speak about tonight. They all suggested European Union. Unhappily I must report that those who advised the subject did not cast much light on its meaning. I think I rather shocked them by replying that I would need to know what is meant by it before I could tell whether I was for it or against it. It is important that people define their terms.

Let me say at once: I do not believe that we shall ever have a United States of Europe in the same way that there is a United States of America. The whole history of Europe is too different.

I do believe however that for nations of the European Community freely to work together and to strengthen their co-operation is just as worthy a purpose. But to submerge their identity and variety would be contrary to the instincts of our peoples and therefore could not bear fruit.

It is on the basis of working towards common goals, of using our strength and influence together, that you will find Britain a strong advocate for a more united Europe.

We want to see greater unity of the Community market,

greater unity of Community action in world affairs, greater unity of purpose and action in tackling unemployment and the other problems of our time, and greater unity in the development and application of new technology. That is what I understand by a united Europe.

These goals are attainable and I believe it is better to work for the substance than to talk of the shadow. There have been so many reports telling us what to do, so many theoretical models. Another report is no substitute for practical progress.

But in 1984 under the presidency of President Mitterrand we have seen more action in solving our practical problems than for many a long year. That is significant not only because of the particular solutions we reached but because if we can solve some difficult problems we can solve others too. In Europe we are beginning to revive the vigour and vitality which once made us the most confident of civilizations.

But although the Community may be at the centre of our common concerns, we must not forget our responsibilities to those who live on the same continent but on the other side of the frontier of freedom. However different our philosophies and way of life, we have a common interest in avoiding armed conflict.

The announcement last week by President Reagan that negotiations are to begin with the Soviet Union on the crucial issues of arms control and reduction is good news for us all, both East and West, and a just return for the patience and purpose which the Alliance have shown.

I would recall to you de Tocqueville's observation that 'of all peoples, those most deeply attached to peace are the democratic nations.' This is an area, Mr Chairman, where Britain and France will need to work even more closely together if, as we hope, substantive negotiations on arms control get under way.

We should also work together to help Europe make a more vigorous and purposeful contribution to the Atlantic Alliance.

For forty years we have enjoyed friendship and security in alliance with an unprecedentedly generous and loyal ally – the United States of America. No nation with such enormous power has ever used it so wisely or with such restraint. But we must never take her commitment to Europe for granted. We must not give the impression that we in Europe want to enjoy the fruits of a *pax Americana* without sharing the costs and risks that make that security possible.

Britain and France are best placed to give a lead. We both maintain an independent nuclear deterrent. Britain keeps 66,000 servicemen fully committed to the Nato Alliance in the heart of Germany, France some 50,000 servicemen just over the border in Germany under its national control. We both have considerable naval forces. We both have a history that has given us interests and responsibilities girdling the world.

Like the US, we both maintain a capacity beyond the Nato area. Let us be proud of it. The security of the North Atlantic countries does not start at the invisible line of the Tropic of Cancer. We can only be truly secure if beyond that line we have ability to protect our trade and other interests and are willing to use it.

European Foreign and Defence Ministers took an important step forward in Rome last month, when they declared their intention of revitalizing the Western European Union.

Such steps are useful. But everything we do must contribute to the strengthening of the overall Alliance. It must never introduce divisions or suspicions into it. For the strength of all is the strength of each.

Europe's defence can also be strengthened by bilateral contacts. Different pairs of countries complement each other in different ways. We in Britain have no reservations about the efforts which France and the Federal Republic of Germany have made to intensify their co-operation. Today, President Mitterrand and I have been talking about what Britain and France for their part can do together. We resolved to give our co-operation a strong political impetus and direction, and to search for areas where we can work together.

Indeed, my discussions with President Mitterrand over the past two days have highlighted the enormous number of fields in which France and Britain *are* working together. We decided at our joint press conference earlier today to set out publicly details of just some of the projects on which Britain and France are collaborating. Some are well known and often in the news. Others are less spectacular, for instance, food technology and bio-technology. And with an eye to the future we have decided to arrange a meeting in London early in the New Year of French and British scientists and technologists to see how we can best co-ordinate our efforts in fundamental and applied research.

No two peoples in Europe have a longer or prouder history as nations than Britain and France. This was recognized by President Mitterrand himself when he said, 'Europe in the abstract, a geometric shape . . . is a caricature. The true Europe needs nations just as a living body needs flesh and blood.'

Mr Chairman, here in France you have the original Statue of Liberty on the Ile des Cygnes in Paris. We also have in the Treaty of Rome a Statute for Liberty. Let us apply that Statute to secure the personal liberty of our people and the free co-operation of our countries in a new European renaissance.

COMMENTARY

One of Mrs Thatcher's greatest triumphs was when, following in the footsteps of Winston Churchill to the same rostrum, she addressed both Houses of the American Congress with a speech of great force and impact. No British Prime Minister since Churchill thirty-three years earlier had addressed Congress, and both the packed chamber and the ovation she received at the end of her speech testified to the regard for Mrs Thatcher in the United States – a country not usually inclined to take great notice of the words of foreign politicians. Moreover, not only did she address Congress; she was repeatedly on television speaking to the American public who find her fascinating not simply because she is a staunch ally but also because she is a woman who has succeeded in the mainly man's world of politics. Asked during one of these interviews whether she agreed with critics who described her as 'tough, credible, honest but also bossy, dictatorial, right wing', she replied: 'It's not for me to judge myself . . . I cannot say what I am like. I only know it took me sixty years to develop and I cannot change now.'

Her speech that day sealed her personal relationship with President Reagan, not least through the Prime Minister's endorsement of his Star Wars (strategic defence) initiative. For one thing, it helped his resistance to Congress defence cuts.

Once again (although she made it clear that the West must maintain disarmament talks with Russia) Mrs Thatcher stated in very clear words what should be the essence of Western policy: 'Let us be under no illusions; it is our strength not their good-will that has brought the Soviet Union to the negotiating table' – and she reminded her audience of President Brezhnev's ominous prediction of the total triumph of Socialism all over the world.

It was a speech of great oratorical skill, often Churchillian in tone, drawing together the changed balance of power in the world and the realities involved in the adjustment of the Western European powers to being in the second rank with only the US and the USSR super-powers in the first. Into this context she also fitted the problems of the Third World, the British reversal of Socialism under her government, and current economic problems. What she said on the last of these subjects, with her warnings about the dangers of protectionism and the burden to other countries arising from the strength of the dollar, implied a degree of criticism of US economic policy at that time which was the more effective for being delivered by a genuine friend rather than by a carping critic. When she returned to London she fell under much criticism from her opponents because President Reagan had just indicated that his administration would not intervene to assist the value of falling European currencies against the over-strong dollar. Nevertheless, Mrs Thatcher's point had been taken and the general tone of her speech was undoubtedly more helpful to future co-operation than pointed criticism would have been. In one very important respect, what she had to say brought future dividends. Her tough remarks about terrorism and the IRA and her stress on her co-operation with the Irish Prime Minister, Garret Fitzgerald, were one step on the road to the eventual agreement of Congress to the extradition of terrorists. This speech was an outstanding exercise in political persuasion.

The United States Congress

WASHINGTON, 20 FEBRUARY 1985

On this, one of the most moving occasions of my life, my first words must be to say thank you for granting me this rare privilege of addressing a Joint Meeting of the United States Congress.

My thoughts turn to three earlier occasions when a British Prime Minister, Winston Churchill, was honoured by a call to address both Houses. Among his many remarkable gifts, Winston held a special advantage here. Through his American mother, he had ties of blood with you. Alas, for me, these are not matters we can readily arrange for ourselves!

Those three occasions deserve to be recalled, because they serve as lamps along a dark road which our people trod together, and they remind us what an extraordinary period of history the world has passed through between that time and ours; and they tell us what later generations in both our countries sometimes find hard to grasp: why past associations bind us so closely.

Winston Churchill's vision of a union of mind and purpose between the English-speaking peoples was to form the mainspring of the West. No one of my generation can forget that America has been the principal architect of a peace in Europe which has lasted forty years. Given the shield of the United States, we have been granted the opportunities to build a concept of Europe beyond the dreams of our fathers; a Europe which seemed unattainable amid the mud and slaughter of the First World War and the suffering and sacrifice of the Second.

When, in the spring of 1945, the guns fell silent, General Eisenhower called our soldiers to a Service of Thanksgiving. In the order of service was a famous prayer of Sir Francis Drake:

> Oh Lord God, when Thou givest to Thy Servants to endeavour any great matter, grant us to know that it is not the beginning but the continuing of the same until it be thoroughly finished, which yieldeth the true glory!

On this day, close to the fortieth anniversary of that service and of peace in Europe – one of the longest periods without war in all our history – I should like to recall those words and acknowledge how faithfully America has fulfilled them. For our deliverance from what might have befallen us, I would not have us leave our gratitude to the tributes of history. The debt the free peoples of Europe owe to this nation, generous with its bounty, willing to share its strength, seeking to protect the weak, is incalculable. We thank and salute you!

Of course, in the years which separate us from the time when Winston Churchill last spoke to Congress, there have been disappointments as well as hopes fulfilled: the continued troubles in the Middle East; famine and oppression in Africa; genocide in South East Asia; the brutal occupation of Afghanistan; the undiminished agony of tortured Poland; and above all, the continued and continuing division of the European continent.

From these shores, it may seem to some of you that by comparison with the risk and sacrifice which America has borne through four decades and the courage with which you have shouldered unwanted burdens, Europe has not fully matched your expectations. Bear with me if I dwell for a moment on the Europe to which we now belong.

It is not the Europe of ancient Rome, of Charlemagne, of Bismarck. We who are alive today have passed through perhaps the greatest transformation of human affairs on the continent of Europe since the fall of Rome. In but a short chapter of its long history, Europe lost the position which it had occupied for two thousand years – and it is your history as much as ours.

For five centuries, that small continent had extended its authority over islands and continents the world over.

For the first forty years of this century, there were seven great powers: the United States, Great Britain, Germany, France, Russia, Japan, Italy. Of those seven, two now tower over the rest – the United States and the Soviet Union.

To that swift and historic change Europe – a Europe of many different histories and many different nations – has had to find a response. It has not been an easy passage to blend this conflux of nationalism, patriotism and sovereignty, into a European Community, yet I think that our children and grandchildren may see this period – these birth pangs of a new Europe – more clearly than we do now. They will see it as a visionary chapter in the creation of a Europe able to share the load alongside you. Do not doubt the firmness of our resolve in the march towards this goal, but do not underestimate what we already do.

Today, out of the forces of the Alliance in Europe, 95 per cent of the divisions, 85 per cent of the tanks, 80 per cent of the combat aircraft, and 70 per cent of the fighting ships are pro-vided, manned and paid for by the European Allies and Europe has more than three million men under arms and more still in reserve. We have to. We are right in the front line. The frontier of freedom cuts across our continent.

Members of Congress, the defence of that frontier is as vital to you as it is to us.

It is fashionable for some commentators to speak of the two super-powers – the United States and the Soviet Union – as though they were somehow of equal worth and equal signifi-cance. Mr Speaker, that is a travesty of the truth! The Soviet Union has never concealed its real aim. In the words of Mr Brezhnev, 'the total triumph of Socialism all over the world is inevitable – for this triumph we shall struggle with no lack of effort!' Indeed, there has been no lack of effort!

Contrast this with the record of the West. We do not aim at domination, at hegemony, in any part of the world. Even against those who oppose, and who would destroy, our ideas, we plot no aggression. Of course, we are ready to fight the battle of ideas with all the vigour at our command, but we do not try to impose our system on others. We do not believe that force should be the final arbiter in human affairs. We threaten no one. Indeed, the Alliance has given a solemn assurance to the world: none of our weapons will be used except in response to attack.

In talking to the Soviet Union, we find great difficulty in getting this message across. They judge us by their ambitions. They cannot conceive of a powerful nation not using its power for expansion or subversion, and yet they should remember that when, after the last war, the United States had a monopoly of nuclear weapons, she never once exploited her superiority. No country ever used such great power more responsibly or with such restraint. I wonder what would have befallen us in Western Europe and Great Britain if that monopoly had been in Soviet hands.

Our task is to see that potential aggressors, from whatever quarter, understand plainly that the capacity and the resolve of the West would deny them victory in war and that the price they would pay would be intolerable. That is the basis of deterrence and it is the same whatever the nature of the weapons, for let us never forget the horror of conventional wars and the hideous sacrifice of those who have suffered in them.

Our task is not only to prevent nuclear war, but to prevent conventional war as well.

No one understood the importance of deterrence more clearly than Winston Churchill, when in his last speech to you he said: 'Be careful above all things not to let go of the atomic weapon until you are sure and more than sure that other means of preserving peace are in your hands!' Thirty-three years on, those weapons are still keeping the peace, but since then technology has moved on, and if we are to maintain deterrence – as we must – it is essential that our research and capacity do not fall behind the work being done by the Soviet Union. That is why I firmly support President Reagan's decision to pursue research into defence against ballistic nuclear missiles, the Strategic Defence Initiative. Indeed, I hope that our own scientists will share in this research.

The United States and the Soviet Union are both signatories to the 1972 Anti-Ballistic Missile Treaty, a treaty without any terminal date. Nothing in that treaty precludes research, but should that research – on either side – lead to the possible deployment of new defence systems, that would be a matter for negotiation under the treaty.

Mr Speaker, despite our differences with the Soviet Union, we have to talk with them, for we have one overriding interest in common: that never again should there be a conflict between our peoples. We hope too that we can achieve security with far fewer weapons than we have today and at lower cost, and thanks to the skilful diplomacy of Secretary Shultz, negotiations on arms control open in Geneva on 12 March. They will be of immense importance to millions. They will be intricate, complex and demanding, and we should not expect too much too soon.

We must recognize that we have faced a Soviet political offensive designed to sow differences among us, calculated to create infirmity of purpose, to impair resolve, and even to arouse fear in the hearts of our people.

Hope is such a precious commodity in the world today, but some attempt to buy it at too high a price. We shall have to resist the muddled arguments of those who have been induced to believe that Russia's intentions are benign and that ours are suspect, or who would have us simply give up our defences in the hope that where we led others would follow. As we learnt cruelly in the 1930s, from good intentions can come tragic results!

Let us be under no illusions. It is our strength and not their good-will that has brought the Soviet Union to the negotiating table in Geneva.

Mr Speaker, we know that our alliance – if it holds firm – cannot be defeated, but it could be outflanked. It is among the unfree and the underfed that subversion takes root. As Ethiopia demonstrates, those people get precious little help from the Soviet Union and its allies. The weapons which they pour in bring neither help nor hope to the hungry. It is the West which heard their cries; it is the West which responded massively to the heart-rending starvation in Africa; it is the West which has made a unique contribution to the uplifting of hundreds of millions of people from poverty, illiteracy and disease.

But the problems of the Third World are not only those of famine. They face also a mounting burden of debt, falling prices for primary products, and protectionism by industrialized countries. Some of the remedies are in the hands of the developing countries themselves. They can open their markets to productive investment; they can pursue responsible policies of economic adjustment. We should respect the courage and resolve with which so many of them have tackled their special problems, but we also have a duty to help.

How can we help? First and most important, by keeping our markets open to them. Protectionism is a danger to all our trading partnerships, and for many countries trade is even more important than aid. And so we in Britain support President Reagan's call for a new GATT round.

The current strength of the dollar, which is causing so much difficulty for some of your industries, creates obvious pressures for special cases, for new trade barriers to a free market. I am certain that your administration is right to resist such pressures. To give in to them would betray the millions in the developing world, to say nothing of the strains on your other trading partners. The developing countries need our markets as we need theirs, and we cannot preach economic adjustment to them and refuse to practise it at home.

And second, we must remember that the way in which we in the developed countries manage our economies determines whether the world's financial framework is stable. It determines the level of interest rates; it determines the amount of capital available for sound investment the world over; and it determines whether or not the poor countries can service their past loans, let alone compete for new ones. And those are the reasons why we support so strongly your efforts to reduce your budget deficit.

No other country in the world can be immune from its

effects – such is the influence of the American economy on us all.

We in Europe have watched with admiration the burgeoning of this mighty American economy. There is a new mood in the United States. A visitor feels it at once. The resurgence of your self-confidence and your national pride is almost tangible. Now the sun is rising in the West.

For many years, our vitality in Britain was blunted by excessive reliance on the state. Our industries were nationalized, controlled and subsidized in a way that yours never were. We are having to recover the spirit of enterprise which you never lost. Many of the policies you are following are the policies we are following. You have brought inflation down. So have we. You have declared war on regulations and controls. So have we. Our Civil Service is now smaller than at any time since the war and controls on pay, prices, dividends, foreign exchange, have all gone. You have encouraged small business, so often the source of tomorrow's jobs. So have we. But above all, we are carrying out the largest programme of denationalization in our history.

Just a few years ago, in Britain, privatization was thought to be a pipe dream. Now it is a reality and a popular one. Our latest success was the sale of British Telecommunications. It was the largest share issue ever to be brought to the market on either side of the Atlantic – some two million people bought shares.

Members of Congress, that is what capitalism is – a system which brings wealth to the many and not just to the few.

The United Kingdom economy is in its fourth year of recovery. Slower than yours, but positive recovery. We have not yet shared your success in bringing down unemployment, although we are creating many new jobs, but output, investment and the standard of living are all at record levels and profits are well up. And the pound? It is too low! For whatever the proper international level of sterling, it is a marvellous time for Americans not only to visit Britain but to invest with her – and many are.

America is by far the largest direct investor in Britain and I am delighted to say that Britain is the largest direct investor in the United States.

The British economy has an underlying strength and, like you, we use our strength and resolve to carry out our duties to our allies and to the wider world.

We were the first country to station cruise missiles on our territory. Britain led the rest. In proportion to our population, we station the same number of troops as you in Germany. In Central America, we keep troops stationed in Belize at that government's request. That is our contribution to sustaining democracy in a part of the world so vital to the United States. We have troops in Cyprus and in the South Atlantic and, at your request, a small force in Sinai. British servicemen are now on loan to some thirty foreign countries. We are alongside you in Beirut; we work with you in the Atlantic and in the Indian Ocean; our navy is on duty across the world. Mr Speaker, Britain meets her responsibilities in the defence of freedom throughout the world and she will go on doing so.

Members of Congress, closer to home there is a threat to freedom both savage and insidious. Both our countries have suffered at the hands of terrorists. We have both lost some of our best young lives and I have lost some close and dear friends. Free, strong, democratic societies will not be driven by gunmen to abandon freedom or democracy. The problems of the Middle East will not be solved by the cold-blooded murder of American servicemen in Lebanon, nor by the murder of American civilians on a hijacked aircraft. Nor will the problems of Northern Ireland be solved by the assassin's gun or bomb.

Garret Fitzgerald and I, and our respective governments, are united in condemning terrorism. We recognize the differing traditions and identities of the two parts of the community of Northern Ireland – the Nationalist and the Unionist. We seek a political way forward acceptable to them both, which respects them both. So long as the majority of people of Northern Ireland wish to remain part of the United Kingdom, their wishes will be respected. If ever there were to be a majority in favour of change, then I believe that our Parliament would respond accordingly, for that is the principle of consent enshrined in your constitution and in an essential part of ours.

There is no disagreement on this principle between the United Kingdom government and the government of the Republic of Ireland. Indeed, the four constitutional nationalist parties of Ireland, north and south, who came together to issue the New Ireland Forum Report, made clear that any new arrangements could only come about by consent, and I welcome too their outright condemnation and total rejection of terrorism and all its works.

Be under no illusions about the Provisional IRA. They terrorize their own communities. They are the enemies of democracy and of freedom too. Don't just take my word for it. Ask the government of the Irish Republic, where it is an offence even to belong to that organization – as indeed it also is in Northern Ireland.

I recognize and appreciate the efforts which have been made by the Administration and Congress alike to bring home this message to American citizens who may be misled into making contributions to seemingly innocuous groups. The fact is that money is used to buy the deaths of Irishmen north and south of the border and 70 per cent of those killed by the IRA are Irishmen – and that money buys the killing and wounding even of American citizens visiting our country.

Garret Fitzgerald – and I salute him for the very brave thing he did yesterday in passing a special law to see that money did not get to the IRA – Garret Fitzgerald and I will continue to consult together in the quest for stability and peace in Northern Ireland, and we hope we will have your continued support for our joint efforts to find a way forward.

Distinguished Members of Congress, our two countries have a common heritage as well as a common language. It is no mere figure of speech to say that many of your most enduring traditions – representative government, Habeus Corpus, trial by jury, a system of constitutional checks and balances – stem from our own small islands. But they are as much your lawful inheritance as ours. You did not borrow these traditions; you took them with you, because they were already your own.

Human progress is not automatic. Civilization has its ebbs and flows, but if we look at the history of the last five hundred years, whether in the field of art, science, technology, religious tolerance or in the practice of politics, the conscious inspiration of it all has been the belief and practice of freedom under law; freedom disciplined by morality, under the law perceived to be just.

I cannot conclude this address without recalling words made immortal by your great President Abraham Lincoln in his second Inaugural Address, when he looked beyond an age when men fought and strove towards a more peaceful future. 'With malice toward none, with charity for all, with firmness in the right that God gives us to see the right, let us strive on to finish the work we are in, to do all which may achieve and cherish a just and lasting peace among ourselves and with all nations!'

Members of Congress, may our two kindred nations go forward together sharing Lincoln's vision, firm of purpose, strong in faith, warm of heart, as we approach the third millennium of the Christian era.

COMMENTARY

International terrorism was the theme of Margaret Thatcher's address to the American Bar Association at a time when it had become increasingly clear that greater co-operation between all civilized and democratic countries was essential if this scourge was to be contained. The Beirut hijacking had concentrated attention as never before on the dangers. A week earlier President Reagan had described an international pattern of terrorism based on the concerted attempt of what he called a 'confederation of terrorist states', Iran, Libya, North Korea, Cuba and Nicaragua, to focus on targets connected with America. The purpose, he claimed, was to disrupt American foreign policy and to remove American influence from those areas of the world where Washington was encouraging stable and democratic government. There was a clear implication in what he said about the ties between these states and Moscow. Arms deals between the Soviet Union and unstable, extremist regimes have damaged international life.

The Prime Minister followed up the President's speech with an appeal for action – 'action to which all countries are committed until the terrorist knows that he has no haven, no escape.' She also suggested that the hijackers should be starved of the media publicity on which they thrive by a voluntary code of conduct adopted by the media. But she laid her greatest stress on the importance of concerted action by those governments with the will to resist terrorist demands.

But, of course, adequate co-operation was not to be forthcoming, and from that lack was to come eventually the American decision to bomb Libya. Thus there was no agreement on the quarantine of Beirut airport which the United States proposed. The European nations talked about terrorism, but they could not bring themselves to act since, in one way or another, almost anything proposed was likely to be inconvenient to the commercial or other interests of some of them. In this speech Margaret Thatcher firmly linked terrorism to other threats to international law, including the growing menace of the drug trade, and she also again spoke of Britain's special experience in Northern Ireland, expressing appreciation for the American President's proposal to ask Congress to ratify an extradition treaty.

The American Bar Association

LONDON, 15 JULY 1985

I am delighted to have this opportunity to welcome on behalf of Her Majesty's Government, and as a member myself of the Bar of England and Wales, this great meeting of the American Bar Association. I hope that your time in the United Kingdom will not be all work and no play.

Perhaps you will make a pilgrimage of professional piety to St Ives in Cornwall, named after the patron saint of advocates. He was renowned for espousing the causes of the poor and the oppressed. In his native Brittany his anniversary is celebrated by a High Mass, at which it is customary to sing this eulogy:

Advocatus quo non latro
Res miranda populo.

A popular translation runs as follows:

An advocate but not a thief,
A thing well nigh beyond belief.

Mr President, no profession is more sadly misunderstood by the public than that of the advocate – unless it be that of the politician. We lead not so much with the chin as with the mouth: *Volenti non fit injuria* would be a complete defence to any complaint that any of us might make.

But the theme of your meeting – Justice for a Generation – is a fit subject for lawyers *and* for politicians. We both have a special responsibility to see that our generation gets justice.

118

For justice to prevail the most basic requirement is the rule of law. It was your Felix Frankfurter who said: 'Limited as law is, it is all that we have standing between us and the tyranny of mere will and the cruelty of unbridled feeling.'

How those words ring out today across a world that is racked by terrorism, hijacking, mob violence and intimidation. How thin is the crust of order over the fires of human appetite and the lust for naked power.

The rule of law has only prevailed for comparatively short periods of history. It exists today in only a small part of the world, of which your country and mine are the centre. We share the Magna Carta. We share the Bill of Rights. We share Habeas Corpus. We share the Common Law. You have enshrined all that we hold dear in that most splendid statement of liberty, the Declaration of Independence.

But the rule of law of itself does not guarantee justice. As Edmund Burke, a most ardent advocate of your cause, put it: 'It is not what a lawyer tells me I may do: but what humanity, reason and justice tell me I ought to do.' That is why the law needs to be fashioned and administered with an awareness of the contemporary concerns of the world outside the court. The law cannot stand separate from the society of which it is part.

This indeed is the frontier on which the politician and the lawyer meet and mingle.

The desire for justice imposes very firm requirements on the politician. First, a recognition that he can never be above the law. Second, his unstinting support for the courts which administer the law and for the police who enforce it. And third, in constructing legislation, his duty to give an honest account of what is practicable and not merely a rhetorical account of what is desirable.

Justice also requires those in public life to repudiate a number of fashionable heresies. The first heresy is that if only a determined minority gather together in large enough numbers to bully or to intimidate others the law either will not, or cannot, be enforced against them. The inference is not only that there is safety in numbers but that this brings with it some kind of collective immunity from legal process. It does not. And it must not. No matter whether those numbers are mobilized by football hooligans, political agitators or industrial pickets: crime is no less crime just because it is committed *en masse*.

A second fashionable heresy is that, if you feel sufficiently strongly about some particular issue, be it nuclear weapons, racial discrimination or animal liberation, you are entitled to claim superiority to the law and are therefore absolved. This is arrogant nonsense and deserves to be treated as such.

It brings me to a third heresy, namely that the law can be obeyed selectively. Those groups who would pick and choose among our laws, obeying some and breaking others, imperil liberty itself. The law must stand as a whole and be obeyed as a whole. 'Liberty is the right to do anything which the law permits,' wrote Montesquieu in 1745, 'and if a citizen were able to do what the law forbids he would no longer have liberty, since all other citizens would have the same ability.'

Mr President, I passionately believe that there is a further prerequisite for justice, and that is democracy. Order we need, but not arbitrary order. This year Britain and the United States celebrate together the fortieth anniversary of the defeat of the Third Reich. It called itself the New Order: order there certainly was, a despotic order with no system of justice independent of the ruling party.

In our own day we can gaze across the brutal Berlin Wall in the direction of those vast land-masses where there is order but no liberty, where there are people's courts but no justice for people. You cannot have justice unless you have the right to challenge the government in the courts. Nor can you have it without the right to change a government and the laws by constitutional means if the majority so desire.

But there is more to democracy than one man, one vote. What good is it to vote unless you are offered a real choice? A choice of views as well as a choice of candidate? After all, Soviet Communism gives everyone the vote. There is no tyranny on earth today which does not make some ritual bow in the direction of universal suffrage.

The foundation of these two great principles, democracy

and the rule of law, is not only the rule of the majority; it is a recognition and acceptance that everyone has a basic right to freedom and to justice, a right which is God-given not state-given, a right so fundamental that no mere government is entitled to take it away.

If we are to obtain the justice for our generation which is the theme of your meeting we must find more effective ways of protecting our citizens from crime. This is not just a matter of giving the police more men and equipment, important as that is. The police cannot do the job on their own. They deserve – and need – our active support. Those who refuse to speak up for them when their support is needed are little better than the carping critics whose voice is so often heard today.

Every one of us has to accept our responsibility as a citizen. No one can opt out.

Mr President, the ease with which we sometimes say 'better 99 guilty men go free than one innocent man be convicted' may make us forget how essential it is to the preservation of ordered and civilized society that the guilty should be convicted and adequately punished.

Our systems are rightly weighted in favour of the accused. But this should not blind us to the fact that the acquittal of a guilty person constitutes a miscarriage of justice just as much as the conviction of the innocent. Such an acquittal exposes law-abiding citizens and the police to more danger – and as always it is the weak who suffer most.

The feeling is also growing in our country – and elsewhere – that some of the sentences which have been passed have not measured up to the enormity of the crimes. This government therefore recently brought before Parliament a Bill including a clause which would have enabled the Court of Appeal to review the appropriateness of a sentence passed in the Lower Court.

Decisions would not affect the sentence in the case in question. But they would give a guide to the kind of sentence which might be expected in similar cases in the future. The procedure was to be used only sparingly. Sadly the Bill did not get through.

I say sadly, because those who so strenuously opposed the Bill appeared to ignore the very real anxiety of ordinary people that too many sentences do not fit the crime.

This issue is not closed. Our constituents are constantly reminding us of the depth and strength of public feeling, and we shall bring the matter back before Parliament so that this concern can be met.

Mr President, for our generation, particularly for our younger generation, there is one further threat to justice which is insidious, dangerous and international. It is the evil of drug addiction and abuse. We can tackle this only if we work together.

I recently raised this at the meeting of the seven Economic Summit countries in Bonn and found that all other leaders, particularly President Reagan, shared my deep concern.

We must act against the grower and producer, through crop eradication; and against the trafficker and the pusher, through the unremitting efforts of customs and police and through tougher sentences, including stripping traffickers of their profits from the sale of drugs.

You already have a law to that effect. We shall introduce one in the next session of Parliament. Together we must attack every link in the chain. And all the time we must never cease to tell young people of the dangers, and help those who have succumbed to climb back to normal life again.

We should bring home the simple moving message of one young girl, eighteen years old, addicted to heroin, cocaine and anything she could lay her hands on. She was crippled from her addiction. She had lost her home, her friends and almost her life. She said: 'It was all such a waste.'

How different from the sight and sound of those marvellous young people of Live Aid in both Wembley and Philadelphia on Saturday who flashed their message of help and hope across the world. That was humanity in action. That was the young people of Britain and America moved by the plight of others thousands of miles away, using the magic of technology to restate in the language of pop the age-old brotherhood of man.

122

We thank and congratulate them for the marvellous lead they gave.

That was the good news.

The bad news is that the same satellites that carried this message had brought home to us only a few days before the savage threat of terrorism. President Reagan made a powerful speech on this issue before your association last week. Here in the United Kingdom we bear its scars and live with its threats every day. The terrorist uses force because he knows he will never get his way by democratic means. In the last fifteen years or so some 2500 of our people have been murdered by terrorists in the United Kingdom. We are grateful for the firm stand which your President and Congress have taken against contributions of money and arms to the IRA. We are also most appreciative of the action of your Administration in inviting Congress to ratify speedily an extradition treaty which will help us bring before the courts those who commit these terrible crimes. That would indeed be justice for this generation.

I repeat, the terrorist uses force because he knows he will never get his way by democratic means. Through calculated savagery, his aim is to induce fear in the hearts of people and weariness towards resistance.

In this evil strategy, the actions of the media are all-important. For newspapers and television, acts of terrorism inevitably make good copy and compelling viewing. The hijacker and the terrorist thrive on publicity: without it, their activities and their influence are sharply curtailed. There is a fearful progression, which the terrorists exploit to the full. They see how acts of violence and horror dominate the newspaper columns and television screens of the free world. They see how that coverage creates a natural wave of sympathy for the victims and pressure to end their plight no matter what the consequence. And the terrorists exploit it. Violence and atrocity command attention. We must not play into their hands.

Mr President, let us make no mistake: the threat from terrorism is growing constantly. The terrorist has access to ever more money. He operates across national boundaries.

Modern technology makes the terrorists' job easier and that of the security forces more difficult.

Now there is a new dimension, brought home to us in the horrific hijacking of your TWA aircraft a few weeks ago: not only an aircraft but an airport was in the hands of hijackers.

Increasingly we see evidence of links between the terrorist groups of different countries. They share funds, training, intelligence and weapons – and a total ruthlessness.

Could anything more clearly point up the need for the governments and security services of all civilized nations to work together against such people? For a victory for terrorism anywhere is a victory for terrorism everywhere.

Nor is terrorism confined to countries where lawlessness and anarchy prevail. Its followers abuse the very freedom of open societies to do their evil work. Where they cannot get their way by the ballot-box they use the bomb. They intimidate or they eliminate those who stand in their way.

The more open our society, the more we must be on our guard. Civilized societies cannot use the weapons of terrorism to fight the terrorist. But we must take every possible precaution to protect ourselves: sustained security measures for our aircraft and our airports; constant checking of people and luggage, however irksome; combined action to penalize countries which harbour and assist terrorists; and above all the closest possible co-operation on pre-emptive intelligence. Too often in the past our countries have begun well but then slackened and grown complacent, making ourselves easier targets.

We have behind us many fine declarations and communiqués of good intent. We need action; action to which all countries are committed until the terrorist knows that he has no haven, no escape. Alas, that is far from true today.

And we must try to find ways to starve the terrorist and the hijacker of the oxygen of publicity on which they depend. In our societies we do not believe in constraining the media, still less in censorship. But ought we not to ask the media to agree among themselves a voluntary code of conduct, a code under which they would not say or show anything which could assist the terrorists' morale or their cause while the hijack lasted?

Most vital of all, we must have the will-power never to give in to the terrorist. Your government and ours are at one on this.

Therefore, let me say: we in Britain will not accede to the terrorists' demands. The law *will* be applied to them as to all other criminals. Prisoners will *not* be released. Statements in support of the terrorists' cause will *not* be made. If hijacked aircraft land here, they will *not* be allowed to take off. For in conceding terrorist demands the long-term risks are even greater than the immediate dangers.

In Benjamin Franklin's words: 'Those who would give up essential liberty to preserve a little temporary safety deserve neither liberty nor safety.' That is the message when dealing with international terrorism: weakness never pays. We would like to see a determination on the part of all countries not to give in to terrorist demands. Once would-be hijackers knew in advance that their purpose would not be served, some of the attractions of their barbarous trade would disappear.

Mr President, the problems of drugs, terrorism and every kind of violence know no boundaries. They remind us vividly of the risks which our open societies face, and the need to control and eliminate them underlines the importance of strengthening international law.

It is now forty years since the United Nations Charter was launched with such high hopes. Yet in that time we have not seen the emergence of an effective and enforceable body of public international law. In relations between countries, justice is still a remote ideal. All too often, might not right prevails. I recall the sombre words of the classical historian who described our world as one where the strong do what they will, and the weak suffer what they must.

In a nuclear world, therefore, it is all the more important that countries stand by the treaties and commitments which they have undertaken.

Particularly important are those treaties between the United States and the Soviet Union which govern their strategic relations: the Strategic Arms Limitation Agreements and the

Anti-Ballistic Missile Treaty. These agreements provide the foundation for our present structure of deterrence on which rest our hopes for peace.

They are the framework within which negotiations to reduce nuclear weapons are taking place in Geneva. That is why I was delighted when President Reagan recently announced his decision that the United States would continue to abide by the Salt Two constraints; and would negotiate on the deployment of any defensive system which may emerge from the SDI research programme in accordance with the terms of the ABM Treaty.

One other treaty deserves special mention, the Nuclear Non-Proliferation Treaty whose Review Conference is held this year. Our two countries were among its principal architects. Signed by nearly 130 countries, four-fifths of the membership of the UN, it has checked the spread of nuclear weapons and helped to make safe the trade in nuclear materials and equipment. You may recall that in the sixties it was widely predicted that by 1985 there would be up to twenty more nuclear weapon states. In fact only one state – not a party to the Treaty – has in that time demonstrated a capacity to detonate a nuclear device. It is vital to our generation that this treaty be preserved and extended to other nations who have not yet signed it.

This is the security we seek, and only the law can provide it. For the law is the condition not only of the survival of nations, but of the maintenance of liberty and justice within nations. Nationally and internationally the law is not only a negative and restraining force, it is a creative and liberating force. It enables the individual, within the framework of order, to exercise his talents freely, in the sure knowledge that the just rewards of those talents will be secure.

As so often, Rudyard Kipling has the last word:

Keep ye the Law – be swift in all obedience –
Clear the land of evil, drive the road and bridge the ford.
Make ye sure to each his own
That he reap where he hath sown;
By the peace among our peoples let men know we serve the
  Lord.

126

COMMENTARY

*The Socialist parties have always joined together internation-
ally to pursue their shared interests. Conservative and centre-
right parties have not done so until recently. But in 1983 the
nineteen member countries of the European Democratic
Union, who had come together to co-ordinate their attitudes
on major European and international issues, were joined by
like-minded parties in Australia, Canada, Japan, New Zealand and the United States to create the International Democratic Union, whose secretariat is currently based at the
Conservative Central Office in London. It was to the IDU
meeting in Washington that Mrs Thatcher spoke in July 1985,
praising the United States as a land of freedom and again
hammering home her theme that responsibility is essentially
individual, not collective.*

*In this speech she acknowledged the changes in the Soviet
Union since Mikhail Gorbachov and a younger and more educated Russian leadership had taken over. But the burden of her
remarks to her fellow Western Conservatives was that the
West should not be taken in by the 'massive propaganda
offensive' that would be mounted in advance of the summit
that was coming in November between President Reagan and
Mr Gorbachov, in which demands would be made on the West
to accept the Soviet view and give up important aspects of*

its own deterrent capacity. But, she insisted, the nature of Communism has not changed and the West must explain its own proposals to their own people in terms which carried conviction and appeal.

Significantly Mrs Thatcher stressed that it was not enough to warn against siren voices. The West must have its own constructive and positive proposals for agreed disarmament. And that, of course, is the essential point. It is vital not to weaken the West's capacity for self-defence. But there would not be sufficient support for nuclear arms in the West if there were not genuine confidence among its informed and free peoples that everything that could reasonably be done for disarmament would be done. The morale of the West depends as much on its self-confidence in its own will for peace as in its determination to defend its freedom. And, although the summit that November was cordial without being fruitful, there have been signs since that some steps forward may be possible.

The International Democratic Union Dinner

WASHINGTON, 25 JULY 1985

Mr Vice-President, from whatever part of the world we come, from whatever country, whatever continent, we all feel that in you we have a particular friend in Washington: someone who knows our countries, someone whose unrivalled experience of government brings an instinctive and sympathetic understanding to our problems, someone who shares and – more importantly – fights for our ideals.

It is of course a great sadness that the President could not be with us. I know that he would not easily be kept away from this first meeting of our International Democratic Union in the United States. But nothing is more important than that he should continue his phenomenal recovery and come back fitter and stronger than ever to give us his leadership. Our message to him and to the First Lady is: 'You have all our affection and best wishes.' And, if I may exploit one of an old actor's best-known lines: 'Don't win this one just for the Gipper, Mr President, win it for all of us.'

To hold this conference in the United States of America is a very special experience for all representatives. Many of us come from countries whose peoples left our shores to come to yours.

Just over four hundred years ago, Sir Walter Raleigh helped to found the first English-speaking settlement in the North

American continent. For him and his companions, and so many like them, America was a land of liberty and opportunity, a land of new beginnings. It has remained so for four hundred years.

In that time, people from many countries have followed. Some have sought and found an escape from tyranny. Others, like Raleigh himself, have sought adventure and the chance to make their fortune.

To them all, the United States has extended a warm and generous welcome – a welcome vividly caught by words inscribed on the Statue of Liberty:

> *Give me your tired, your poor,*
> *Your huddled masses yearning to breathe free,*
> *Send these, the homeless, tempest-tost to me,*
> *I lift my lamp beside the golden door!*

The United States is still the land of liberty – but more than that. You have flourished because from your early days liberty has been indissolubly linked with responsibility, with endeavour, with self-reliance.

Nor would you have survived without giving a helping hand to one another, accepting that success brought, not greater privilege, but greater obligations.

These values which we share and admire, you enshrined in that most marvellous expression on liberty – the Declaration of Independence.

We must recall these things and relearn their lessons. One, that those who would enjoy the fruits of liberty must first assume its obligations. Have we not all heard politicians – not of our own way of thought – conveying the impression that somehow the standard of living comes from governments and not from personal effort? And that somehow someone else will pay for all the good things for which electors are invited to vote. It was George Bernard Shaw who said: 'Freedom incurs responsibility; that is why so many men fear it.'

And a second lesson we must constantly keep before us is that democracy is about more than the rule of the majority. It is a recognition and an acceptance that everyone has a basic right to freedom and justice. That is why we are meeting here today, as we talk about contemporary problems against the background of fundamental values.

Liberty has brought not only dignity, but prosperity undreamed of by our forefathers. It is that which has enabled the West to bring hope and help to millions of African citizens who have suffered famine.

No shadow of complacency occupies our minds as we dine tonight in the same world. But we are proud to live in a society which can keep food flowing to those stricken areas, and proud that our young people used their freedom to raise millions of dollars for humanity.

Tackling famine in the world is a great challenge. So too is the maintenance of peace.

All of us have very much in mind the importance of the summit meeting which will take place at the end of November between the President and Mr Gorbachov. We must not underestimate the changes which are taking place in the Soviet Union. A younger generation has made its way into the seats of power, a generation that is more highly educated, which has a more sophisticated understanding of the importance of image and presentation. We have seen it in Mr Gorbachov's walk-abouts. We have seen it in the greater use of press conferences and briefings – always for highly selected information. We have heard talk of economic reform.

These new techniques are bound to be employed this autumn in a massive propaganda offensive aimed at public opinion in our countries. Would that we could get through as easily to theirs. Our peoples will be presented with the alluring prospect of large reductions in nuclear weapons, of a stable peace just round the corner if only . . . If only the United States were to give up the SDI. If only Britain and France were to abandon their nuclear deterrents, even though they are only a tiny proportion of Soviet forces. If only we were to accept Soviet proposals which would preserve and guarantee Soviet superiority in numbers. If only in other words we accept the Soviet view and give up our own.

131

It will be our task to keep our people aware of the realities. The reality that the nature of Communism has not changed even if its image has been touched up. The reality that the new brooms in the Soviet Union will not be used to sweep away Communism, only to make it more efficient – if that can be done. The reality that the defence of the West for many years will continue to depend upon deterrence through nuclear weapons. The reality that those who are now in leading positions in the Soviet Union have never known anything but Communism. They do not think in any other terms. Their view of the world will remain dominated by their ideology.

But it will not be enough just to warn against siren voices. We must have a positive approach, firm, clear and constructive proposals of our own – for substantial reductions in nuclear weapons, for a ban on chemical weapons, for increasing East–West contacts – and explain them to our people in terms which will carry conviction and appeal. We must show that our commitment to negotiation, our commitment to peace is more honest and more credible than the specious proposals of the other side. Our parties, members of the IDU, will have a special responsibility in this.

At this conference we have reasserted our fundamental beliefs.

Today we can look to the future with confidence. We are winning the battle of ideas, and the values in which we believe belong to all generations.

COMMENTARY

While President Reagan was offering 'a new start' in realistic terms to the Soviet Union, Mrs Thatcher was telling the United Nations in very plain terms what was wrong with it. She paid tribute to its achievements, to its capacity to set the stage for negotiations (as in the Middle East), to its peace-keeping role and to its special agencies. But without mincing her words she also accused it of double standards, and in terms that were prescient in view of the turn of events in the summer of 1986, she specifically accused it of double standards in its attitude to South Africa.

While it was right to condemn South Africa for its degrading treatment of black people, it was also right to offer not rhetoric and abuse but positive encouragement when steps were taken in the right direction. Such encouragement, she clearly indicated, was lacking from the United Nations in respect of South Africa — partly because there were nations in the UN which harboured terrorists and in other ways did not live up to the United Nations' proclaimed standards.

Perhaps her most telling point was her reference to the propensity to pass judgement on countries, not on the merits of the case, but because it was easy to find a majority against them. Since then (while other more totalitarian regimes go uncensured) the power of political fashion has made it ever harder to view South Africa logically, and almost impossible to stand out against sanctions without risking the accusation of defending apartheid. The steps that have been taken in South Africa to end social apartheid have been ignored, and the Commonwealth majority has adopted the position that nothing short of negotiations for one man, one vote in a unitary state will be accepted as an alternative to escalating sanctions.

For resisting this Mrs Thatcher has been vilified. Yet it is clear that full-scale sanctions will only stiffen Pretoria against further liberalization, and are more likely to lead to, than to prevent, an increase in bloodshed. Moreover, a substantial weight of liberal opinion in South Africa, including Mrs Helen Suzman and many businessmen who support democracy, believe that sanctions will not work and that South Africa can withstand them. What is needed is progress by agreement, which can never be achieved simply by threats. The aim must be to provide a lasting sense of security among all the people of South Africa, including the whites who form nearly 20 per cent of the population. It is the lack of that security which has now driven the whites into rigidity, and for this much blame lies with those who wish to use sanctions to force the kind of total surrender which, rightly or wrongly, the white South Africans believe will lead to the one-party state predominant elsewhere in Africa. Among self-styled progressive opinion, the wind of facile moral fashion and the obsession with one man, one vote, blows aside a cautious concern for the kind of advance which is as peaceful and bloodless as possible. It is a wind of fashion which owes much more to the ability to muster an easy, emotional or conventional majority, than to a moral position based on reason and the facts of the case.

The General Assembly of the United Nations 40th Commemorative Session

NEW YORK, 24 OCTOBER 1985

On this celebration of the fortieth anniversary of the United Nations, I should like to start with the words of someone who was present at its creation, Winston Churchill. In his Fulton speech in 1946 he said:

> We must make sure that the United Nations work is fruitful; that it is a reality and not a sham;
> that it is a force for action, and not merely a frothing of words;
> that it is a true temple of peace in which the shields of many nations can some day be hung, and not merely a cockpit in the Tower of Babel.

And so I shall address my remarks today to the work of the United Nations.

The United Nations' work *has* been fruitful over those forty years. It has acted as a court of world opinion. And now no government can afford to neglect or to ignore its views. The Security Council has given us a forum for managing both the unexpected crisis and the stubborn problem. The General Assembly provides a setting where the voice of any member country, however small, can be heard. In the Secretary-General we have an impartial and skilled negotiator in whom we have total confidence and trust.

The United Nations has also shown that it is a force for action. It can help to keep the peace in three vital ways. First, by setting the stage for negotiation, as it did with the famous Resolution 242 on the Middle East. Second, by acting as a catalyst which persuades those in dispute to prefer negotiation to confrontation. And third, by pursuing its peace-keeping role. Had it not been for the blue helmets and blue berets of the United Nations – guided by a great British servant of the United Nations, Brian Urquhart – local conflicts would have spread, and the toll of death and the flood of homeless would have been even greater.

But there are those who refuse to make their fair financial contribution to these vital peace-keeping operations. I believe they are failing in their duty to the United Nations, to mankind and to peace. I think it is about time they felt guilty that they leave others to bear an unfair share of the burden.

I pay tribute to those specialized agencies, which have concentrated on their appointed task: for example eliminating disease, caring for the needs of children, feeding and sheltering refugees. They and the men and women who serve them deserve all our thanks.

In these ways the United Nations has shown that it is a reality and not a sham; it is a force for action, not a mere frothing of words; it is a temple of peace, not just a Tower of Babel. For all its dangers, our world is safer and more orderly thanks to the United Nations.

It would be easy on this anniversary simply to praise and to express support. But if we really mind about the United Nations – and I am one of those who do – then we must make it more effective by recognizing its shortcomings and putting them right.

We have to admit to many disappointments. As so many speakers have said today, it is true we have been spared the ultimate horror of another world war. But that is little consolation to the many millions of people who have been killed, maimed or made homeless in over one hundred and forty lesser conflicts.

And we still cannot say that basic human rights – freedom of speech and opinion, freedom from arbitrary arrest, freedom from torture – are observed across the world. The problem is not a lack of rules and standards: they are all there in the United Nations Charter and in the Universal Declaration on Human Rights. The problem is that some governments blatantly disregard these standards because human rights have no place in their political system.

May I say that resolutions of the United Nations have not always been objective. Some have been guilty of double standards. Judgement has been passed on countries not on the merits of the case but because it was easy to find a majority against them. Other countries who have deserved censure have been protected through sheer political expediency. South Africa is properly condemned for its degrading refusal of basic human rights to black people. Yet where are the resolutions on the treatment of Soviet Jewry?

Nor has the United Nations yet shown the capacity to deal effectively with terrorism. The terrorist is callously prepared to kill, cripple and wound to get his own way. He speaks the language of human rights even as he extinguishes them by his deeds.

Mr President, at the United Nations we have spoken out against terrorism often enough. And yet there are countries represented among us which harbour and train terrorists; and others who seem ready to support terrorism in preference to peaceful negotiation. This is an utter betrayal of our Charter.

Order and an effective rule of law are just as important to justice between nations as they are to justice within nations. But alas in forty years, although we have created a corpus of public international law, we have not been able to make it effective and enforceable. In some nations justice is still a remote ideal.

If the majority in the United Nations wants to influence the government of a particular member, it must offer not rhetoric and abuse but encouragement when steps are taken in the right direction. I refer in particular to South Africa, where there is a sense that the time for change has come. Provided that negotiations are accompanied by a suspension of violence by all sides, I believe that there is a chance of progress – progress which will allow all the people of South Africa, of whatever colour or creed, to play their rightful part in the government of their country in conditions of prosperity and peace.

What are the reasons for the disappointments and shortcomings of the United Nations? Why do we hear cynical assertions that the United Nations has ceased to be relevant; that all it does is to pass resolutions; that disputes brought before it are prolonged and not resolved; that collective action by such a disparate body of nations will of necessity always be weak and ineffective?

I think the answer is twofold. Wishful thinking has led some people to believe that the United Nations was intended to be a kind of World Government. Well, it may be a kind of parliament of the world but it is not and never can be a government of the world. Its structure limits what it can do.

Second, when we ask about shortcomings we should start by looking at ourselves. The United Nations is only a mirror held up to our own uneven, untidy and divided world. And if we do not like what we see, there is no point in cursing the mirror; we had better start by reforming ourselves.

Our task after forty years is to rediscover both the hope and the resolve that characterized the founding of the United Nations.

First we must recognize that in most circumstances the power of international organizations in today's world is the power of persuasion, not coercion. The United Nations cannot and should not try to dictate detailed solutions to countries involved in disputes. Only the parties themselves can reach agreements, whether they be the Soviet Union and the United States, the Arabs and the Israelis, or white and black in Southern Africa.

We must also recognize that it is not enough to agree on words. We must live up to them. Nor should we take refuge in deliberate ambiguity, in finding 'a form of words' because that is easier than finding a solution. No lasting solution will be achieved by saying one thing and meaning another, or by getting a majority for a resolution only because the words are capable of meaning different things to different nations. We must decide what we mean. And say so.

As in our own nations, so with the United Nations, we have a duty to maintain the effectiveness and efficiency of the whole system and to get better value for the money we spend. The work of the agencies should not be side-tracked into political issues which are none of their business. Unesco is an example of this, which is one reason why we have given notice of our intention to withdraw. Political issues belong to this Assembly. Technical bodies are for technical issues.

Mr President, we cannot do without the United Nations. But we can do a lot more with it. There are plenty of new areas where international action is required and where the United Nations can take a lead. We have taken action on a global scale to deal with the famine in Africa – action led by the nations which run free enterprise economies. They are the ones able to provide food and help for the starving.

We must take more action to end the international drugs trade, that traffic in death which ruins so many young lives. We must try to stop the cultivation of plants from which these drugs are made. We must intercept the transport of them and catch and punish severely the criminals responsible for their sale. Governments – all governments – must co-operate whole-heartedly in this task.

And I believe we must be more resolute in our action to deal with international terrorism. The murders of an American and a Soviet diplomat in the last month remind us that no country is immune. We should all recognize that in dealing with terrorism weakness never pays.

These are problems against which national efforts alone are not enough.

As the idealism and freshness which accompanied the birth of the United Nations have been tested in the school of life, it was inevitable that we should suffer disappointments. But let us not lament what has gone wrong. Let us learn from it. It was once again Winston Churchill who expressed so well the positive approach we need, in his description of the Journey of Life:

Let us be contented with what has happened to us and thankful for all that we have been spared.

Let us treasure our joys but not bewail our sorrows.

The glory of light cannot exist without its shadows.

Life is a whole and good and ill must be accepted together.

Let us continue to work together until the United Nations is a true temple of peace in which the shields of many nations can be hung.

COMMENTARY

Probably no other single issue has aroused more public controversy than the decision to allow the Americans to use British bases from which to fly in their bombing raid on Libya. There was widespread understanding of the Americans' purpose: to strike against one of the countries which nourish international terrorism. But when the effects of the raid were seen on television, particularly the killing of ordinary people including children, they inevitably caused distress, and there was also considerable criticism of the reasoning which led to the raid. In this speech to the House of Commons, the Prime Minister set out her reasons for agreeing to the Americans' request, and once again her judgement was fundamentally determined by the principle of deterrence – that it is essential for terrorists to know that firm steps will be taken against them to deter them from attacking others. Because it seemed very possible that it might not have that effect, many thought that the American action was misguided.

The case that was made against the American bombings was not that they would lead to Libyan reprisals, the murder of hostages (though they did, in the Middle East) or even the death of civilians. The criticism was that the bombings did not have a clear logic. For if terrorism still continued from Libya, would more raids follow, and if so how many? If terrorism were bombed out of Libya and concentrated in countries already hardly less guilty in the Middle East, would these terrorist bases also be bombed as well, irrespective of the international consequences? Or was the raid on Libya, and perhaps one or two more thereafter, to be considered as a punitive strike in isolation, and largely designed to satisfy American public opinion?

The impracticability of pursuing the same tactics in the Middle East was the reason for many misgivings about the American raid. But there was no doubting the strong grounds for Margaret Thatcher's co-operation. For one thing, there was the debt we owed America for aid in the Falklands conflict. But the decisive justification was the Prime Minister's proper concern for the Western Alliance, which had undoubtedly been strained by the refusal of other European nations to co-operate in collective action against terrorism. There was a risk of growing American isolationism.

Clear evidence existed of Libyan involvement in terrorism, of which the Prime Minister was able to give the Commons information in her speech. On those grounds, the raids were certainly justified. This was one of the most complex issues and decisions to face Western leaders. It split public opinion, but there should be no doubt that the criterion by which the decisions were taken was the right one: deterrence.

The House of Commons Debate on Libya

LONDON, 16 APRIL 1986

My statement yesterday explained the government's decision to support the United States' military action, taken in self-defence, against terrorist targets in Libya.

Of course, when we took our decision we were aware of the wider issues and of people's fears. Terrorism attacks free societies and plays on those fears. If those tactics succeed, terrorism saps the will of free peoples to resist.

We have heard some of those arguments in this country: 'Don't associate ourselves with the United States,' some say. 'Don't support them in fighting back; we may expose ourselves to more attacks,' say others.

Terrorism has to be defeated; it cannot be tolerated or side-stepped. When other ways and other methods have failed – I am the first to wish that they had succeeded – it is right that the terrorist should know that firm steps will be taken to deter him from attacking either other peoples or his own people who have taken refuge in countries that are free.

The United States' action was conducted against five specific targets directly connected with terrorism. It will, of course, be for the United States government to publish their assessment of the results. However, we now know that there were a number of civilian casualties, some of them children. It is reported that they included members of Colonel Gaddafi's own family.

The casualties are, of course, a matter of great sorrow. We also remember with sadness all those men, women and children who have lost their lives as a result of terrorist acts over the years – so many of them performed at the Libyan government's behest.

As I told the House yesterday, since May 1984 we have had to advise British citizens choosing to live and work in Libya that they do so on their own responsibility and at their own risk. Our consul in the British interests section of the Italian embassy has been and will remain in close touch with representatives of the British community, to advise them on the best course of action.

Terrorism thrives on a free society. The terrorist uses the feelings in a free society to sap the will of civilization to resist. If the terrorist succeeds, he has won and the whole of free society has lost.

We are most grateful for the work of the Italian authorities, as our protecting power, on behalf of the British community in Libya.

In this country, we have to be alert to the possibility of further terrorist attacks – so, too, do our British communities abroad. Our security precautions have been heightened, but it is, of course, the technique of the terrorist not just to choose obvious targets. Members of the public should therefore be ready to report to the police anything suspicious that attracts their attention. We have also taken steps to defend our interests overseas, seeking from foreign governments enhanced protection for British embassies and communities.

The United Nations Security Council met twice yesterday and resumes today. With some significant exceptions, first international reactions have been critical, even to this carefully limited use of force in self-defence, but I believe that we can be pretty certain that some of the routine denunciations conceal a rather different view in reality.

Concern has been expressed about the effects of this event on relations between East and West. The United States informed the Soviet Union that it had conclusive evidence of Libyan involvement in terrorist activities, including the Berlin bomb, that limited military action was being taken and that it was in no way directed against the Soviet Union.

We now hear that Mr Shevardnadze has postponed his meeting with Mr Shultz planned for next month. I must say that that looks to me like a ritual gesture. If the Soviet Union is really interested in arms control it will resume senior ministerial contacts before long.

Right Hon. and Hon. Members have asked me about the evidence that the Libyan government are involved in terrorist attacks against the United States and other Western countries. Much of this derives, of course, from secret intelligence.

As I explained to the House yesterday, it is necessary to be extremely careful about publishing detailed material of this kind. To do so can jeopardize sources on which we continue to rely for timely and vital information.

I can, however, assure the House that the government are satisfied from the evidence that Libya bears a wide and heavy responsibility for acts of terrorism.

For example, there is evidence showing that, on 25 March, a week before the recent Berlin bombing, instructions were sent from Tripoli to the Libyan People's Bureau in East Berlin to conduct a terrorist attack against the Americans. On 4 April the Libyan People's Bureau alerted Tripoli that the attack would be carried out the following morning. On 5 April the bureau reported to Tripoli that the operation had been carried out successfully. As the House will recall, the bomb which killed two people and injured 230 had exploded in the early hours of that same morning.

This country too is among the many that have suffered from Libyan terrorism. We shall not forget the tragic murder of WPC Fletcher by shots fired from the Libyan People's Bureau in London just two years ago tomorrow. It is also beyond doubt that Libya provides the Provisional IRA with money and weapons. The major find of arms in Sligo and Roscommon in the Irish Republic on 26 January, the largest ever on the island, included rifles and ammunition from Libya.

There is recent evidence of Libyan support for terrorism in a number of other countries. For instance, only three weeks ago intelligence uncovered a plot to attack with a bomb civilians queueing for visas at the American embassy in Paris. It was foiled and many lives must have been saved. France subsequently expelled two members of the Libyan People's Bureau in Paris for their involvement.

On 6 April an attempt to attack the United States embassy in Beirut, which we know to have been undertaken on Libyan government instructions, failed when the rocket exploded on launch.

It is equally clear that Libya was planning yet more attacks. The Americans have evidence that United States citizens are being followed and American embassies watched by Libyan intelligence agents in a number of countries across the world. In Africa alone, there is intelligence of Libyan preparations for attacks on American facilities in no fewer than ten countries.

There is other specific evidence of Libyan involvement in past acts of terrorism, and in plans for future acts of terrorism, but I cannot give details because that would endanger lives and make it more difficult to apprehend the terrorists. We also have evidence that the Libyans sometimes chose to operate by using other Middle East terrorist groups.

But we need not rely on intelligence alone because Colonel Gaddafi openly speaks of his objectives.

I shall give just one instance. In a speech at the Wheelus base in Libya in June 1984, he said: 'We are capable of exporting terrorism to the heart of America. We are also capable of physical liquidation and destruction and arson inside America.' There are many other examples.

Yesterday many Hon. Members referred to the need to give priority to measures other than military, but the sad fact is that neither international condemnation nor peaceful pressure over the years has deterred Libya from promoting and carrying out acts of terrorism.

In 1981 the United States closed the Libyan People's Bureau in Washington and took measures to limit trade with Libya. Later, in January this year, the United States government announced a series of economic measures against Libya. They sought the support of other Western countries. We took the view, together with our European partners, that economic sanctions work only if every country applies them. Alas, that was not going to happen with Libya.

In April 1984 we took our own measures. We closed the Libyan People's Bureau in London and broke diplomatic relations with Libya. We imposed a strict visa regime on Libyans coming to this country and we banned new contracts for the supply of defence equipment and we severely limited Export Credits Guarantee Department credit for other trade.

Over the years, there have been many international declarations against terrorism – for example, by the economic summit under British chairmanship in London in June 1984; by the European Council in Dublin in December 1984; and finally by the United Nations General Assembly in December 1985. All those meetings adopted resolutions condemning terrorism and calling for greater international co-operation against it.

Indeed, the resolution of the United Nations General Assembly unequivocally condemns as criminal all acts, methods and practices of terrorism. It calls upon all states, in accordance with international law, to refrain from organizing, instigating, assisting or participating in terrorist acts in other states. After the *Achille Lauro* incident, the Security Council issued a statement condemning terrorism in all its forms everywhere.

But while resolutions and condemnation issued from those cities, in others more terrible events – bombings, hijackings and kidnappings – were happening or were being planned. They are still being planned.

It was against that remorseless background of terrorist atrocities, and against the background of the restrained peaceful response, that the case for military action under the inherent right of self-defence to deter planned Libyan terrorist attacks against American targets was raised.

President Reagan informed me last week that the United States intended to take such action. He sought our support. Under the consultation arrangements which have continued under successive governments for over thirty years, he also sought our agreement to the use of United States aircraft based in this country. Hon. Members will know that our agreement was necessary.

In the exchanges which followed, I raised a number of questions and concerns. I concentrated on the principle of self-defence, recognized in article 51 of the United Nations charter, and the consequent need to limit the action and to relate the selection of targets clearly to terrorism.

There were of course risks in what was proposed. Many of them have been raised in the House and elsewhere since the action took place. I pondered them deeply with the ministers most closely concerned, for decisions like this are never easy. We also considered the wider implications, including our relations with other countries, and we had to weigh the importance for this country's security of our Alliance with the United States and the American role in the defence of Europe.

As I told the House yesterday, I replied to the President that we would support action directed against specific Libyan targets demonstrably involved in the conduct and support of terrorist activities; further, that if the President concluded that it was necessary, we would agree to the deployment of United States aircraft from bases in the United Kingdom for that specific purpose.

The President responded that the operation would be limited to clearly defined targets related to terrorism, and that every effort would be made to minimize collateral damage. He made it clear that, for the reasons I indicated yesterday, he regarded the use of F111 aircraft from bases in the United Kingdom as essential. There are, I understand, no other F111s stationed in Europe. Had we refused permission for the use of those aircraft, the United States' operation would still have taken place; but more lives would probably have been lost, both on the ground and in the air.

It has been suggested that, as a result of further Libyan terrorism, the United States might feel constrained to act again. I earnestly hope that such a contingency will not arise. But in my exchanges with the President, I reserved the position of the United Kingdom on any question of further action which might be more general or less clearly directed against terrorism.

Moreover, it is clearly understood between President Reagan and myself that, if there were any question of using United States aircraft based in this country in a further action, that would be the subject of a new approach to the United Kingdom under the joint consultation arrangements.

Many Hon. Members have questioned whether the United States' action will be effective in stopping terrorism or will instead have the effect of quickening the cycle of violence in the Middle East.

Let us remember that the violence began long ago. It has already taken a great many lives. It has not been so much a cycle of violence as a one-sided campaign of killing and maiming by ruthless terrorists, many with close connections with Libya. The response of the countries whose citizens have been attacked has not so far stopped that campaign.

Indeed, one has to ask whether it has not been the failure to act in self-defence that has encouraged state-sponsored terrorism. Firm and decisive action may make those who continue to practise terrorism as a policy think again.

It has also been suggested that the United States' action will only build up Colonel Gaddafi's prestige and support in the Arab world. In the very short term, one must expect statements of support for Libya from other Arab countries – although one is entitled to ask how profound or durable that support will be. But moderate Arab governments, indeed moderate governments everywhere, have nothing to gain from seeing Colonel Gaddafi build up power and influence by persisting in policies of violence and terror.

Their interest, like ours, lies in seeing the problems of the Middle East solved by peaceful negotiation, a negotiation whose chances of success will be much enhanced if terrorism can be defeated.

Let me emphasize one very important point. A peaceful settlement of the Arab–Israel question remains our policy and we shall continue to seek ways forward with moderate Arab governments. Indeed, I shall be seeing King Hussein later this week to discuss this very matter.

The United States is our greatest ally. It is the foundation of the Alliance which has preserved our security and peace for more than a generation. In defence of liberty, our liberty as well as its own, the United States maintains in Western Europe 330,000 servicemen. That is more than the whole of Britain's regular forces. The United States gave us unstinting help when we needed it in the South Atlantic four years ago.

The growing threat of international terrorism is not directed solely at the United States. We in the United Kingdom have also long been in the front line. To overcome the threat is in the vital interests of all countries founded upon freedom and the rule of law.

Terrorism exploits the natural reluctance of a free society to defend itself, in the last resort, with arms. Terrorism thrives on appeasement.

Of course we shall continue to make every effort to defeat it by political means. But in this case that was not enough. The time had come for action. The United States took it. Its decision was justified, and as friends and allies, we support it.